MW01045974

Winning with the

BOSS

FROM HELL

Books by Shaun Belding:

Winning with the Boss from Hell
Winning with the Employee from Hell
Winning with the Customer from Hell

Winning with the
BOSS
FROM HELL

A GUIDE TO LIFE
IN THE TRENCHES

SHAUN BELDING

ECW PRESS

Copyright © Shaun Belding, 2004

Published by ECW PRESS
2120 Queen Street East, Suite 200, Toronto, Ontario, Canada M4E 1E2

All rights reserved. No part of this publication may be reproduced, stored in a retrieval
system, or transmitted in any form by any process — electronic, mechanical,
photocopying, recording, or otherwise — without the prior written permission
of the copyright owners and ECW PRESS.

NATIONAL LIBRARY OF CANADA CATALOGUING IN PUBLICATION

Belding, Shaun
Winning with the boss from Hell : a guide to life in the
trenches / Shaun Belding.

(Winning with the... from Hell series)
ISBN 1-55022-632-0

1. Managing your boss. I. Title. II. Series: Belding, Shaun
Winning with the... from Hell series.

HF5549.12.B43 2004   650.1´3   C2003-907313-0

Cover and Text Design: Tania Craan
Cover photo: Getty Images
Production and Typesetting: Mary Bowness
Printing: Transcontinental

This book is set in Akzidenz Grotesk and Minion.

The publication of *Winning with the Boss from Hell* has been generously
supported by the Canada Council, the Ontario Arts Council, the Government of Canada
through the Book Publishing Industry Development Program. Canadä

DISTRIBUTION
CANADA: Jaguar Book Group, 100 Armstrong Avenue, Georgetown, ON, L7G 5S4
UNITED STATES: Independent Publishers Group, 814 North Franklin Street,
Chicago, Illinois 60610

PRINTED AND BOUND IN CANADA

ECW PRESS
ecwpress.com

This book is dedicated to Margo, Lee, and Jackie.
I am so *the boss of you.*

For Lewis Carroll and the Children

The gentle journey jars to a stop;
The drifting dream is done.
The long-gone goblins loom ahead.
The deadly, we thought were dead;
Stand waiting everyone.

— Walt Kelly

CONTENTS

GO TO HELL, GO DIRECTLY TO HELL, DO NOT PASS GO. . . .

Abandon all hope, all ye who enter here.
— Dante's *Inferno*

Once you factor in small details such as sleeping, eating, commuting, peeing, bathing, and those sorts of things, the average person spends more than half his adult life in his place of employment.

Ew.

Now imagine spending that half of your life with a boss who is an ignorant, foul, rude, selfish, loud, obnoxious, abrasive, incompetent, impatient, incoherent, embarrassing, harassing, condescending, indecisive, dirty, smelly, mean-spirited, sexist, wimpy, vindictive, unappreciative, crude, credit-stealing games master. And those are his *good* points.

Double ew.

If you happen to be one of those people unfortunate enough to work for one of these Bosses from Hell, it may make you feel better to know that you're not alone. Type "Bad Boss" into the Google search engine, and you'll get over six million hits — they can't all be about the same person. A study of 1,800 employees by Australian management consulting firm Dattner Grant identified that more than three-quarters of Australian workers are dissatisfied with the leadership of those running their companies. Denver-based company Delta Road surveyed 700 employees and found 81% classifying their immediate supervisor as a "lousy manager." There is even a Web site named "killourboss.com." Nope, you're not alone out there, and the scary part is that it's global and getting worse, not better.

So what's going on? Are bosses just getting more stupid? Have grouchiness and insensitivity been identified by the HR gods as core competencies for management? Has Harvard opened a new school of management for the ethically and morally challenged? Or are we just becoming a nation of oversensitive whiners?

Although Bosses from Hell have been around for as long as there have been bosses, I think the apparent Boss from Hell epidemic can be attributed to the convergence of a number of factors. Higher productivity expectations, higher workloads, higher stress levels, and lack of training have all played a role in the way people are behaving. As perhaps has always been the case, many bosses simply don't have the necessary competencies, having been promoted to their positions for the wrong reasons — they've been around the longest, they've been superstar salespeople, they've been in the right place at the right time, that sort of thing. Some of them also have to deal with Bosses from Hell of their own.

However they came to be, it doesn't diminish the

impact they can have on us and on the companies we work for. A study in Buckinghamshire Chilterns University College in London showed how people's blood pressure levels change in the presence of a supervisor. The results were dramatic, with people's blood pressure increasing with "unfair" bosses and decreasing with "fair" bosses. A startling Finnish study illustrated how people who have high job strain or feel little reward from their hard work are twice as likely to die of a heart attack or stroke than colleagues rewarded regularly and treated reasonably. In their book *First, Break All the Rules: What the World's Greatest Managers Do Differently*, Marcus Buckingham and Curt Coffman detail one of the largest Gallup studies ever conducted, which suggests that no amount of pay or employee training can compensate for a bad boss. They confirm the adage that "People join great companies, but they leave because of bad managers."

Bad management doesn't seem to be restricted to any one level or industry. You can find Bosses from Hell from low-level supervisory positions right up to CEOs. They exist across the board through trade, retail, manufacturing, service, professional, public, and private sectors. Ironically, some of the scariest stories I've heard have come from the health care and education sectors — areas charged with sustaining physical and mental health.

One of the biggest reasons that Bosses from Hell are so

stressful is that there is no real way to prepare for them. They come in so darned many flavors, and they can often show up so unexpectedly, that we are frequently caught off guard. One of my company's clients once called me to tell me the exciting news that his boss, an aggressive and abusive director, had been transferred out of his division. The better news was that his boss was being replaced by a woman my client had known for years, and, although he had never worked for her, he liked her a lot. "She's incredibly positive. I've never seen her in a bad mood. She always has a nice thing to say to people."

It didn't take long for the glow to wear off, however. He soon discovered that, as nice as she was, she was virtually incapable of making a decision. She would postpone every decision until the last minute, forcing her employees to feel as though they were continually scrambling through weekends and late into the night to try to meet deadlines. To make matters worse, she would often change her mind midway through the panicked rush, forcing employees to scrap countless hours of hard work. My frustrated client, burned out with a dozen stalled projects in the works, quit eight months later.

Further magnifying the impacts of Bosses from Hell is the sense of helplessness we get from the position power they hold. We fear repercussions if we try to address their unpleasant behavior, and this fear can be stronger and more immediate than the misery they create. Some bosses actually count on this fear and use it to control employees. It is a very effective technique for them. After all, they control our wages, the projects we work on, the hours we work, the people we work with, and our opportunities for advancement. Even when we think about looking elsewhere for employment, they are the people our prospective new employers will be calling for references. It is very easy to feel trapped, with no place to turn and no one to turn to.

With the proper planning and the right attitude, however, it is possible to change this feeling of helplessness and regain control over your happiness and your future. *In Winning with the Boss from Hell*, we will look at a broad cross-section of bad bosses and some effective ways of dealing with them. We'll crawl inside the dark crevices of their minds to find out what sorts of things make them tick and why they expect us to tolerate their behavior. We'll look at some of the more common and often self-destructive responses to Bosses from Hell that inevitably lead to lose-lose situations. The goal of this book is to help you recapture that half of your life you spend at work and take the residual stress away from the other half that is supposed to be your own.

We'll also look at how our own perspectives color our perceptions of our bosses. A boss whom you believe to be micromanaging, for example, may be perceived by other people as being on top of things and providing timely feedback. If you believe that younger, less experienced people don't make good bosses, you might become resentful when having to report to a younger manager. You may have negative predispositions about people's gender, race, ethnicity, or previous work experience.

Poor employer-employee relationships are often a self-fulfilling spiral that we unwittingly create ourselves. A new boss takes over, and you have some reservations about him. Your boss senses your discomfort in the way you say and do things and notes that you have a bit of an attitude. He responds to your attitude with a little of his own. When this happens, you say to yourself "I *knew* I wasn't going to like this guy," and the battle is on. You now think of yourself as having a Boss from Hell, and he thinks of himself as having an Employee from Hell. Which one of you is right? Maybe both, maybe neither. The important thing to remember is that, to break any negative cycle like this, one of you has to take the initiative and make an effort toward positive change.

It's also important to remember that if you just go by your gut — if you simply react to situations as they happen — it is very unlikely that you will generate any long-term, positive solutions. You need a plan. You need to identify what the real problems are and what course of action you can take to create the best results. Solving Boss from Hell issues rarely involves a quick fix. Chances are that what makes these people into Bosses from Hell has been developing in their evil little brains for a long time. Be prepared to be both persistent and consistent in your approach.

The benefits of learning how to deal with a Boss from Hell cannot be understated. Work, that place where you're spending up to half of your life, becomes a more enjoyable place. The stress stops spilling into your personal life, and you find yourself having more fun outside the workplace. You become more confident and productive as you begin to realize that you have greater control over your destiny than you thought you did. Believe it or not, you might even begin to get along with your Boss from Hell. Even come to like him. Honest — it happens. We are all just people, after all, and with a little effort you might discover some common ground. It's worth a shot, and it beats the hell out of the alternatives.

PART ONE

WHAT THE HELL?

We to the place have come, where I have told
thee, thou shalt behold the people dolorous,
who have foregone the good of intellect.

— Dante's *Inferno*

CHAPTER ONE

PSYCHICS 101: READING BOSSES' MINDS

Whether or not you succeed every time you try is less important than whether or not you try every time.

A senior HR manager I know told me the story of a district manager who once loudly berated her team. "You guys are nothing to me," she said to them. "I could have you replaced by a team of monkeys — and they'd probably do a better job." Another story I heard was of a boss at an assembly plant who would just help himself to a different employee's lunch from the refrigerator every day. The employees all knew it, but everyone was afraid to do anything about it. He didn't try to hide it — he referred to it as the "daily special." There's an owner of a retail chain I know who used to randomly fire people just to keep store employees on their toes.

It's hard to believe that these kinds of people even exist. It's hard to understand why somebody actually hired them in the first place. It's nearly impossible to comprehend why, at some point in time, someone would make the conscious decision to promote these people to positions of authority.

How does this happen? How is it that these Bosses from Hell, some of them with genuine personality disorders, got to where they are today? Sometimes the answer is obvious — he's the owner of the business, for example. He promoted himself to the position of boss from the outset, and for you it was just a bad decision to take a job with him. Sometimes it's bosses' sons or daughters, who, because they've never run the real risk of being fired, have never had the inclination to concern themselves with how to become better managers.

Many other factors may have come into play in bringing your Boss from Hell to where she is today. Following are a few.

1. *Tenure*: This is probably the number one reason that Bosses from Hell get to where they are today. They've simply been around the longest. They know all the systems, they know everybody's name, and they've never been quite bad enough to fire. They may have absolutely no skills or aptitude for management, but they do have seniority.

2. *Good at Something Else − the Halo Effect*: How many times have you seen somebody promoted simply because she was good at something else? Retail, hospitality, and call center industries are notorious for doing this. They take their best servicepeople and promote them to positions of managers and supervisors. They neglect to take into account that the skill sets of a good serviceperson may be entirely different from those of a

good manager. It's an easy mistake to make. Decision makers are looking for someone who knows the business — someone with a positive track record of meeting or exceeding expectations and someone they know they can trust. "How big a transition could it possibly be to turn this person into a manager?" they think. Sometimes it's impossible.

3. *Experience*: Many people are promoted to the position of boss because they have a lot of experience in the industry. Maybe they worked for a competitor, a supplier, or a customer. That kind of experience can often blind people to significant shortcomings in management skills. It's amazing how many people mistake experience for aptitude when hiring.

4. *Whom They Knew*: That old saying "It's not what you know but who you know" is frequently true. Often people get a job because they know the manager or have some kind of relationship with the person doing the hiring.

None of these, of course, is the right reason for someone being promoted to boss. The thing is, though, these bosses don't realize they have been promoted for the wrong reasons. I can honestly say that, among all the substandard bosses I have met in my training and consulting business, not one perceives himself as being in his position for the wrong reasons. Just once I would like to hear one of them say "Yeah, I got the job because my buddy Frankie is the vp. I'm pretty crappy at what I do, and there are a dozen people here who could do the job better than me." I don't think that will ever happen.

Once you've figured out how these people get to where they are, the next question is why do these bosses behave so badly? How is it that behavior that seems so appropriate and obvious to us just seems to elude them?

In many cases, Bosses from Hell simply have a poor understanding of what the role of "boss" really is. They're like the dog who chases cars but wouldn't know what to do if he ever caught one. Your boss got the job but really doesn't have a clear understanding of what to do. He doesn't know how to give you direction; he doesn't know how to plan things. All he knows is that he has certain productivity targets to meet and that he is supposed to make sure his team somehow meets them.

Perhaps he himself hasn't had good role models. If his experience has been with bosses who were self-centered and manipulative, he may well believe that bosses are supposed to act this way. He may believe that a good manager is supposed to be serious and grouchy all the time. He may think that, if he's not being a task master, he's not doing his job properly. Many times, too, outside circumstances affect his behavior. He may be tremendously overwhelmed at home (not to mention at work). Not everyone reacts well under stress.

There are three fundamental things that contribute to most Boss from Hell behavior: *motivation*, *expectations*, and *personality*.

Motivation

In the menswear store where I often go to buy my clothes, there is a wonderful salesman I deal with named Jack. He's been working in that store for almost 20 years, and in his tenure he's seen a number of managers come and go. Not only do I consider Jack a great salesperson, but he also has all of the qualities I would ascribe to an excellent manager. He is upbeat, positive, and knowledgeable, and he has high standards for himself and those around him.

When I asked Jack why he had never taken on the role of manager, he shrugged and said "They keep asking me, and I keep saying no. I'm a salesman — that's what I do. That's what I like. I make good money in salaries and commissions, and when I go home at night I can completely push work out of my head. The managers here are often taking work home with them. They have to hire and fire people, go to meetings, set schedules — I like things just the way they are." There are a lot of people like Jack who are very comfortable in what they do and aren't particularly motivated to move any further up the ranks.

What is it, then, that motivates people to take on the additional stress that comes with managerial positions? It's important to think about because you can gain a lot of insight into your Boss from Hell when you understand why he took the position in the first place.

A number of things inspire people to move into management. Many people, for instance, are very title-driven. They're attracted to the prestige that comes with the position, and for them the title of "manager" signifies accomplishment and success. Other people are attracted to the increased power and control that come with management positions. They like to be in charge, and they calculate their value by how many people report to them. Some are just driven to be at the top. They have a competitive nature and like to win. They are goal seekers and are continually setting their sights higher. Still others are driven to positions of management because they believe it's expected of them. Their friends or family members are in similar roles. They may have spouses who are pushing them. But, ultimately, the most common and compelling driver is good old-fashioned money. In most businesses, the higher you move up in management, the more you earn. So management becomes the logical option for people who are seeking more and better things for themselves.

These motivating factors can give us great insight into some of the causes of bad behavior. A money-driven boss whose team is falling short of productivity targets may become grouchy if his performance bonus is in jeopardy. A boss driven by power and control needs might become frustrated when his level of authority doesn't equal his level of responsibility. A boss driven by prestige can respond badly if he thinks he isn't being given the respect that his title warrants.

Give some thought to the behavior of your boss. Has she left you any clues that might help you to determine her motivation for becoming a manager? The better you understand this basic drive, the better you will understand what might trigger her unreasonable behavior.

Expectations

If motivation is the fuse to the Boss from Hell bomb, then the boss's expectations of you are the things that can light that fuse. There are many reasonable expectations that your boss might have of you, and living up to those expectations becomes your part in the employer-employee contract. Following are six key expectations.

Communication

If your Boss from Hell is one who always seems to make poor decisions, you may want to consider that perhaps it's because she is receiving insufficient information. A large factor in the quality of the decisions we all make has to do with both the quantity and the quality of the information we receive. You may decide, for example, to allow your 16 year old to go to a party on a Friday night.

Your decision is based on your knowledge of your child and the friends who will be at the party. Another parent, however, with different information, may consider your decision quite foolish. He may know that there will be drugs or alcohol at the party. Or he may know of another group of kids planning to attend who might be an unwholesome influence on your child. You could end up looking stupid and irresponsible, when all you really were was uninformed.

If it is, in fact, a case of your boss having insufficient information, it could be that she simply doesn't try to seek it or doesn't pay attention to the sources that she does have. But there are a number of other potential reasons. Perhaps she herself has a Boss from Hell who doesn't communicate well. Maybe employees aren't getting their reports in on time or are fudging them to make them look better. You yourself might be partly to blame for your boss's lack of information. Are you making an effort to communicate effectively with your boss, or are you typically waiting for her to come to you?

Compliance

A boss expects you to do the tasks you're asked to do — get your paperwork done on time, fulfill your sales goals, reach certain productivity levels, etc. I'm always amazed at how many employees are unable to grasp this basic concept. I remember once helping a company launch a massive national customer service campaign. As part of it, we were going coast to coast conducting customer service seminars and workshops to frontline employees. It was a certification process, and participation was mandatory.

In virtually every market we visited, one or two employees elected not to participate in either the class-room training or the in-store coaching sessions. Some, of course, had legitimate reasons for not attending, but others had no real reasons other than they simply didn't want to go. The store managers were held accountable for any employees who didn't attend, and monthly bonuses were held back if a team's attendance was unsat-isfactory. It was easy to see how some of the managers became a little grouchy when their employees didn't show up as instructed.

I've heard stories about a hospital night cleaning crew who routinely slept three to four hours each shift, then got upset when they were fired. The union for a retail grocery chain on the West Coast filed a grievance because management listed "smiling" as an expectation of customer service employees.

The thing is, if your boss wants you to do something, make sure you have solid, valid reasons before you choose to ignore him. Compliance is pretty basic stuff, really. As long as the task falls within the boundaries of your job, just do it. If you want your boss to become unpleasant, don't do it.

Support

Managers also expect you to support the initiatives that they put in place even if you don't agree with them.

"In my last performance review, my manager wrote that I wasn't a team player," one call center CSR once complained to me bitterly. "It was totally unfair," he continued. "Just because I hate those dorky little contests he's always running doesn't mean I'm not a team player!" In discussions with the manager afterward, I discovered that the CSR not only disliked the "dorky little contests" that the manager ran, but also publicly made fun of them, often making sarcastic remarks to the other team members. A boss's job of motivating people and driving performance is often made more difficult by employees who seem to actively work against those ends. When a manager perceives that someone is not being supportive either to him or to the team, he has to take action.

An acquaintance of mine, Allan, has been coaching junior hockey for a number of years. As a head coach, he prefers a very exciting, offensive playing system. His teams are typically involved in high-scoring games, and they win more often than they lose. Currently, however, he is working as an assistant coach with a head coach who favors a more cautious, defensive style.

I had the opportunity recently to watch Allan before a game working with his forwards. He was passionately expounding the virtues of playing a strong defense and sticking to their system. To hear him, you'd think there was simply no other way to play the game of hockey.

"I hate this trap! [the name for the defensive system they were playing]" he confided in me later. "It is such a boring way to play the game!" You'd never know it by the way he worked with the players. But he understood that there was a time to lead and a time to follow, and it was his time to follow. Imagine what would have happened if Allan had decided to voice his opinions to the players or, worse, actively promote his favored style of play. Not only would the team have suffered, but the head coach would also have become incredibly frustrated.

Support is essential for managers and becomes a rarer and more valuable commodity the higher up a manager gets. The further up the corporate food chain someone is, the fewer avenues there are for support, feedback, or collaboration. In your job, for example, you can turn to written guidelines or any number of people — coworkers, bosses, etc. — to provide you with sug- gestions regarding the decisions you have to make and feedback on your performance level. The closer you get to senior management, however, the fewer of these resources you have, and usually those peers are focused on different aspects of the business.

A CEO's job, for instance, bears out the old adage "It's lonely at the top." As the CEO of a company, you have no peers. You might have a senior management team to bounce ideas off, but you're never quite sure if they are agreeing with you because they think the ideas are good or because they're trying to please you. The information you do get has usually been filtered through several layers of people and may be presented to you in such a way that it paints an inaccurate picture. Unless you happen to be in one of those companies that has an effective 360° feedback process in place, you really have no way of knowing objectively how well you're doing your job. And, for a CEO, there is the harsh reality that the buck genuinely stops with you. There is no safety net in place in case you make a bad decision.

While your boss may not have quite the challenges of a CEO, she still may be under a significant amount of stress. The pressure can come in a variety of forms, and responses to those pressures can range from virtually nothing to near pathological. Many people, as I've mentioned, deliberately avoid management positions for that very reason — they don't want to deal with the pressures and responsibilities.

Your boss makes a lot of decisions, and in all fairness you can't expect to be happy with every one. The only way a team can function is if everyone supports all of the decisions — even the unpopular ones. If you really want to have everything exactly the way you like it all the time, then start your own business. Otherwise, when you're in somebody else's boat, you row in the direction you're told to row.

Effort

Even if sometimes you aren't able to comply with what your boss wants you to do, or if you somehow slip in your support, most bosses will give you the benefit of the doubt if they believe you are making a genuine effort. Whether or not you succeed every time you try is less important than whether or not you try every time. Most bosses prefer to have an employee who tries her hardest and fails occasionally than one who tries only some of the time.

Attitude

Many things are beyond our control. We can't control how smart we are, how tall we are, how good looking we are, etc. And we can't control the external things that impact our lives. The one thing that we do have absolute, complete control over, however, is our attitude. We can choose to be nice or nasty, conciliatory or confrontational, angry or agreeable. A positive attitude impacts not only your performance but also the performance of the entire team. We've all seen situations where one person's negativity has brought everybody else down.

Negative people are rarely conscious of their negative attitudes. And some are very adept at giving themselves permission to be negative. For example, have you ever met someone who has told you "I'm a very honest person, and I say what's on my mind"? Inevitably, this is a person who regularly says negative things about the company and other people. Under the guise of being "honest," she creates a negative atmosphere that impacts everyone she works with.

A positive attitude means looking for the best in things and in people. It means looking beyond problems to embrace opportunities and challenges. It means making an effort to be a positive influence on those around you. People with positive attitudes make a difference in the lives of those around them and the companies they work for. Not coincidentally, I've discovered that the people with positive attitudes also have dramatically fewer challenges with their bosses.

It may be unrealistic for a boss to expect every employee to be energetic, enthusiastic, bouncy, and bubbly. It is fair, though, for her to expect at the very least a positive attitude.

Results

When a boss has set goals or targets for employees that are fair and attainable, it's reasonable for her to expect results. Sure, sometimes we all miss our performance targets. And sometimes we're faced with external forces beyond our control. But those situations should be the exceptions, not the norm. It is, after all, ultimately a boss's job to ensure that employees produce results. And a boss who doesn't do this, although a nice person, isn't really doing her job well. *Effort*, as we discussed earlier, is critical. But, ultimately, *results* are what we are all accountable for.

These six things — communication, compliance, support, effort, attitude, and results — represent the core of every boss's expectations. When a boss perceives that you aren't delivering substantially on any one of them, and that your behavior is impacting her ability to achieve the goals that motivate her, conflict in some form is inevitable. The encouraging part is that these elements are all very controllable. If you find that you are lacking in any one of them, you may want to focus on changing your own behavior to see how your boss responds.

Personality

If motivation is the fuse, and the boss's expectations of you are the things that can light that fuse, then personality is the factor that determines the nature of the explosion. How a boss responds to failed expectations will be largely dependent on his personality. You can't change his personality, of course, but working to understand it may help you to predict and prepare for his behavior.

There is a great variety of Bad Boss personality types, many of which are outlined in Chapter 12, "Stupid Boss Tricks — and How to Beat Them." In general terms, however, Boss from Hell personalities fall into three basic categories: *aggressive*, *passive*, and *manipulative*.

Aggressive

The aggressive Boss from Hell is the boss whose "fight or flight" mechanism always defaults to fight. These bosses are the predators of the working world — the sharks. Following are some of the symptoms of an aggressive personality.

- When something goes wrong, their first instinct is to look for blame and then to punish the person they have selected.
- They become defensive when someone presents a differing point of view and will try to squash that point of view through argument, ridicule, or an attack of their own.
- They are focused entirely on their own thoughts and needs and are insensitive to those of others.
- They prefer intimidation over cooperation.

The aggressive Boss from Hell uses sticks instead of carrots. He rarely rewards performance; instead, he creates an atmosphere in which people are afraid to fail — a fear that works effectively to dampen independent thought and creativity. He prefers employees who are deferential and subservient and feels threatened by assertiveness. If he has an employee who also has an aggressive personality, he will use his position power to drive him away.

A look into the sea world can give us some clues into the best method for dealing with an aggressive boss. Take the spiny and poisonous blowfish, for example. For the most part, they are gentle and nonthreatening. They go about their business and don't go out of their way to bother anyone else. Predators, however, avoid blowfish, knowing there is a price to pay for trying to snack on them. It's a defensive strategy, and, like the blowfish, you should have a strong defense mechanism in place to avoid being bitten. Chapter 4, "Covering Your Butt 101," outlines some effective defense mechanisms.

Passive

The passive Boss from Hell nearly always chooses flight over fight. He shies away from conflict as well as decisions. Unlike the aggressive predator sharks, he is more like the sea coral, patiently waiting for things to come to him. While the aggressive boss makes you feel defensive and substandard, the passive boss fills you with frustration and a sense of helplessness. His inability to make tough decisions (and sometimes easy ones) slows operations down to a crawl and can create roadblocks to your success. Following are some of the symptoms of passive personality bosses.

- They avoid making decisions until the last minute.
- When there is conflict in the office, or if there is a difference of opinion between team members, they ignore it and hope it will go away.
- They will not stand up to their bosses even if they believe those bosses are wrong.
- They rarely stand behind their employees when things go wrong.
- They back down in the face of strong-willed or aggressive employees.
- They rarely take any disciplinary action, and when they do they have usually been pushed by their bosses.
- They avoid taking risks at all costs.

The passive Boss from Hell has worked very hard at developing a Teflon coating. He is typically insecure and avoids being put in positions in which he might be held accountable for actions or decisions. He has learned through experience that most things will just blow over if he ignores them long enough. The passive behavior is his way of making sure that his butt is covered. He depends on strong, self-motivated team members to drive projects forward.

The most effective way of working with the passive Boss from Hell is to adopt a "Better to beg forgiveness than ask permission" philosophy. When you think about it, because of his Teflon coating, anything that goes wrong is going to fall on your shoulders anyway. You might as well do your best to ensure that things go right.

What this means is that instead of saying "Hey, boss, we have a problem here; should we try to fix it?" you should say "Hey, boss, I just wanted to let you know that I fixed this problem." Because of his passive nature, he won't likely give you a lot of grief for your actions. You have to be prepared, however, to be hung out to dry if things go wrong. No matter — you'd be hung out to dry anyway.

If you have coworkers you trust and respect, it never hurts to run the actions you're going to take past them before you do anything. They may not be there to stand behind you if things go sideways, but they can at least provide you with some input and alternative opinions. One caution if you take this approach: if your boss does challenge your actions, don't refer to the coworker you consulted. Your boss's response will invariably be "Why would you consult with Charlie instead of me?" Unfortunately, overly passive bosses rarely recognize their ineffectiveness and become offended if they think they have somehow been circumvented.

Manipulative

The manipulative Boss from Hell is perhaps the most

dangerous of creatures. She is like the deep-sea angler-fish, which has a glowing lure hanging in front of its face that attracts fishes and other deep-sea animals. Its prey never know what hits them.

The manipulative boss is the classic wolf in sheep's clothing — an aggressive personality shrouded in a passive shell. She is nonconfrontational but tremendously controlling. She rarely takes actions that are not calculated and self-serving. Following are some of the traits of manipulative bosses.

- You are often unsure what their real agenda is.
- They often go behind your back.
- They are overly suspicious.
- They build alliances with senior managers and team members and use these alliances to retaliate against anyone who challenges them.
- They can be sweet and deferential to somebody's face and then disparage him behind his back.

The techniques they use are diverse, but the most common is manipulation through loaded questions and statements. Here are some examples.

1. John, a retail employee, forgets to mention the company's loyalty card to a customer. The manipulator says "John, you didn't offer the customer one of our cards. I assume it is because you don't believe in

the value of them." John, who simply forgot, is now in a defensive position where he has to affirm his belief in the cards and confess his error.

2. Susan, the manipulator's executive assistant, fails to copy one of the team on a memo. The manipulator says "Do you not think Linda should be included?" Susan now feels stupid.

3. Bob tells the manipulator that he thinks a project isn't going as smoothly as it could. In the next team meeting, the manipulator says "Bob seems to believe that you people aren't doing a good enough job." Bob is now in the awkward position of looking like a troublemaker.

The manipulator often has an uncanny way of bringing people into his confidence and then subtly using the information against them. He presents things in such a way that people are forced to take certain positions. The scary part is that he's usually able to do so without looking bad himself.

Dealing with a manipulative Boss from Hell is tricky. If you take an assertive or aggressive stance, she will don her sheep costume and plead innocent. "I'm sorry you've become defensive" is the sort of thing she might say. "I certainly was not suggesting. . . ." If you take a passive stance of your own and try to ignore her, you'll end up playing right into her hands. Your backing down is the response, in fact, that she's looking for.

The best method, albeit a somewhat dangerous one, is to subtly try to beat her at her own game. Challenge her challenges with the same passive-aggressive questioning style. In our first example, where the manipulator says "John, you didn't offer the customer one of our cards. I assume it is because you don't believe in the value of them," your response could be "Why do you assume that, just because I forgot, I don't believe in the cards?" The question now puts the manipulative boss in the defensive position of having to justify her assumption. She now has to take a more direct posture and remind John not to forget to sell the cards. Manipulators don't like having to be direct.

Mild sarcasm (emphasis on *mild*) can also be effective. Take our second example, in which Susan failed to copy a team member on a memo and the manipulator said "Do you not think Linda should be included?" Susan could reply with a smile: "Aw, you caught me. You're right — I was trying to keep Linda out of the loop." Again the manipulator now has to be direct and say "Well, I think you should put her back in the loop."

When manipulators begin to recognize that you won't become defensive with their tactics, they will begin to deal with you a little more directly. And, as long as they don't perceive you as taking an aggressive stance, your working relationship will become a little more positive.

It is important to have some understanding of your boss's personality type, as well as her motivation and expectations, if you want to learn how to cope with her reactions. If you watch her for a while, you'll begin to recognize patterns in her actions that can give you great insight into what to expect from her. On the surface, your boss may appear unpredictable and volatile, but beneath it all you'll find some consistent elements that contribute to her behavior. Having a better understanding of your boss may not make her any nicer, but it can make her easier to work with.

CHAPTER TWO

COMMON YET VERY BAD STRATEGIES

It's like playing chicken with a brick wall.
Even when it's a tie, you lose.

I think the hardest part of having a Boss from Hell is that very few resources are available to you for dealing with him. You can turn to friends and coworkers for advice, but their expertise in winning with these kinds of conflict is rarely greater than yours. Your HR department, if your company has one, can be of help, but it is restricted in the kind of advice it can provide. Often you are left with only two options: just suck it up or quit.

No, when it comes to winning with Bosses from Hell, we're pretty much left to our own devices. We work on instinct and respond to situations the best way we know how. Unfortunately, though, many of the strategies we use are not only ineffective but also sometimes painfully counterproductive. The official term, I believe, is "CLMS": Career-Limiting Moves.

CLMS are usually a product of speaking or acting before thinking. Our Boss from Hell says or does something stupid, and we respond by saying or doing something even more stupid. We throw gasoline into the fire in our boss's eyes. We openly question his judgment or motives. We defy rules and ignore instructions. We forget that, while the boss isn't always right, he's still always the boss.

Many years ago I had the opportunity to watch a shopping center marketing director conduct a virtual clinic in CLM foot-shooting. She was relatively new to that shopping center, with just under a year's tenure, and she reported to a general manager whom she considered to be grossly ineffective. In her brief employment with this center, she'd managed to rack up success after success with promotions and advertising. The tenants all loved her, and so, it seemed, did the people in her head office. To all appearances, she could do no wrong.

Emboldened by her success and the accolades she was receiving by her head office and her peers, she began to openly show her disdain for her boss. She began to miss important management meetings. She sent out e-mails to her GM, openly questioning his judgment, with cc's to people in the head office.

She began to suspect something was wrong when she stopped being invited to senior management meetings and when one of the VPs quietly removed her from his joke e-mail list. The bombshell hit two weeks from her one-year anniversary. The GM walked into her office with a big empty box, set it down on her desk, and said, simply, "You're fired. Clean out your desk. If you want to talk about it, I'll be in my office."

A few minutes later, after she had collected herself, she walked into her GM's office and found him sitting there with the same VP who used to send her the funny e-mails. "They told me I wasn't a team player," she said to me afterward. "They had a whole laundry list of all the stupid things I had said and done over the past few months. I felt numb, standing there, as I realized that I had orchestrated my own unemployment."

Years have passed, and she is now able to look at what she did and laugh at herself. She even managed to reconcile with her former GM. The two of them are working together again in a different shopping center, this time with a much healthier relationship.

There are five kinds of CLMs you should try to avoid.

CLM 1: Public Embarrassment

We can think whatever we want about our Bosses from Hell in private, but when we're in public it is important that we keep our game faces on. If you strongly disagree with a decision your boss made, or something he said, discuss it with him in private. Never bring it up publicly, or it might come back to haunt you.

I remember a manager telling me, after a training session, of his belief in a collaborative management style. One of his employees who was standing within earshot fired back with "Sure, but you take all the credit when things go right!" This obviously had been a bone of contention between the manager and that employee, and the manager was mortified that he had brought it up in public and in front of me. The look the manager gave him was scary. "CLM" I thought to myself as I smiled at them.

It's also not a good idea to correct your boss in front of other people unless it is absolutely necessary. As an example, here are some excerpts from a conversation I once had with the president of a financial company and his executive assistant. The president was trying to give me a broad overview of the company and some of the challenges it was facing. The executive assistant seemed to be intent on calling him on all of his facts.

President: The company has about five hundred employees.

Assistant: Four hundred and eighty-five.

President: The company has been in business since 1972.

Assistant: Technically, it was 1970.

President: The company has grown a lot over the last few years, but morale, overall, is pretty good.

Assistant: Not really. This place is a stress factory.

President: We've introduced a lot of new products this year.

Assistant: Nine. Not as many as last year.

This went on for about half an hour, until the president stood up and said "Shaun, can we continue this conversation at a later time? Say, Thursday over lunch? Rose, can I see you in my office please?" I never saw her again.

Why were the corrections bothering him? Because they were unimportant to the conversation. When you feel the need to correct your boss in public, it's a good idea to first ask yourself "How important is this really?" and "Is my boss going to appreciate it?"

CLM 2: Being Confrontational

There is a big difference between confronting someone, which we will talk about later in the book, and being confrontational. Confronting someone is an assertive position. Being confrontational is an aggressive position. Confronting your boss might mean going into his office after a meeting and saying "You know what, boss? I really didn't appreciate being singled out in the meeting like that." Bringing up that fact during the meeting by saying something like "Hey, why are you singling me out?" would be confrontational.

Being confrontational with your boss, particularly if he is a Boss from Hell, forces him to become defensive. It forces him into a me-versus-you position, and it's rarely a good strategy. While getting it all out might make you feel better in the short term, in the long term you're almost guaranteed to lose.

clm 3: Threatening

Anytime you put your boss in a position where he feels defensive, it's a Bad Thing. Anything you might do or say, therefore, that your boss might perceive as either a direct or an indirect threat is something to be avoided. A direct threat to your boss — e.g., "If things don't change around here, I'm going to quit," threatening to go over his head, or threatening to get a group of colleagues to unite against him — only serves to polarize the situation. In taking such actions, you make it clear that it is officially a him-versus-you situation, which only fuels the ongoing challenges you're having. He may now feel the need to defend himself against what he perceives to be an attack. Even worse, he may feel the need to go on the offensive.

Indirect threats will have the same effect. While not an open declaration of war, they still make your boss feel threatened. He begins to notice that you've started to use butt-covering cc's on your e-mails and memos. He notices you spending more time with the district manager when she drops by for a visit. You begin noticeably documenting things you never before documented. Little warning bells start to go off in your boss's head, and things that were bad with him now become worse.

Like all of us, your Boss from Hell has a survival instinct. When he feels threatened, his fight-or-flight mechanism kicks in. Given his position power, his greater experience, and his probable better connections within the company, it's a no-win situation for you. It's like playing chicken with a brick wall. Even when it's a tie, you lose. Threatening a boss definitely rates as a CLM.

CLM 4: Psychoanalyzing

There are a lot of people who like to categorize everyone they meet into personality types. They like to pigeonhole people based on their first impressions. You'll often hear these people say things like "Oh, yes, I know the type" or "I've worked with that type before." It seems to give us a certain amount of comfort to believe that we have a grasp on the world around us and a sense of control in our encounters with other people.

Sometimes these pigeonholes are based on convenient stereotypes, giving us a feeling of superiority over the people around us. "He's just another guy with a Napoleon complex" I often hear employees say about demanding bosses who are shorter than average. "He's one of those guys who's always got his way by bullying" employees say about managers who are larger than average. "He's got a bean-counter mentality" others will say of a manager with a financial background. "She's just another woman trying to overcompensate" some will say of an assertive female boss.

Pigeonholing, or stereotyping, is a defensive strategy we often use when faced with a boss or manager we don't see eye to eye with. The problem with pigeonholing is that, once we've convinced ourselves that someone is a certain type, we typically close our minds to any of that person's other attributes. It's a bad strategy at best, and it becomes a CLM when you decide to voice your opinions to your boss.

"You know, just because I'm not black doesn't mean I'm going to work less hard for you" I once heard someone say to her African-American boss, whom she assumed to be sensitive to racial issues. Race wasn't a big deal for him, and he was more than a little offended that his employee had made that assumption. I once sat in a senior management team meeting and heard one of the executives say to the president "I know you're thinking that a woman can't do this job, but I still recommend Sylvia." The president bristled at the suggestion that gender had even entered into the deliberations. I remember a call center CSR once saying to her supervisor "I expected you to do that. You're a deflector. That's what deflectors do." The supervisor, although not quite sure what her employee meant, was pretty sure it wasn't a compliment.

Nobody likes being pigeonholed, second-guessed, or psychoanalyzed — especially by an employee. It hints at disrespect and creates an uncomfortable working relationship.

CLM 5: Hiding

There is a fascinating strategy that some people use to avoid being confronted by their bosses or to avoid certain types of work. They hide. They try to avoid or deflect the issues. Think, for instance, of the salesperson who hasn't met her targets for the month. She knows that her boss is going to be asking why. She doesn't really want to face him, so she creates a diversion. When she comes into the office, she acts distraught over some personal crisis. Her sister, daughter, mother, or some other family member is sick. Something horrible has happened to a close friend. Her boss, feeling sorry for her, decides to postpone the talk about her performance. Mission accomplished. I once watched a district manager put off firing a retail store manager for almost six months because she didn't want to add stress to the manager's life — which seemed to be perennially in crisis.

There are many different ways to hide from people or situations you don't like. You can call in sick. You can take breaks at convenient times. You can immerse yourself so deeply in something else that people don't want to disturb you. Hiding can be an effective avoidance technique, but eventually people will start to see through it. Once your boss realizes what's going on, it's a definite CLM.

The thing about CLMs is that they are all self-inflicted and, as such, are all entirely preventable. You just have to think before you act or speak. Think about the potential consequences of everything you do, and ask yourself if they're really worth it. The fewer CLMs you commit, the fewer challenges you will have with your Boss from Hell.

CHAPTER THREE

FINDING YOUR HAPPY PLACE

Having pride in your work is something that nobody can ever take away from you – not even the Boss from Hell.

Before we go into more detail about specific actions you can take to deal with the Boss from Hell, let's look at some of the things that you can control that will minimize the negative impact the Boss from Hell has on your workday. While the Boss from Hell may always remain a Boss from Hell, with a few techniques you can reduce the amount of bad boss behavior directed specifically toward you.

Hot Buttons

We all have hot buttons. And your boss may have any one of several that can trigger bad behavior. There are some buttons, however, that you can push to trigger positive behavior, and they can go a long way toward improving your work relationship with your boss.

Many years ago we were told that cholesterol was a bad thing. Recently, it was discovered that certain types of cholesterol in fact foster healthy living. Hot buttons are like cholesterol. Some will save you, and some will kill you. We've discussed some of the killers, but there are three good ones that work almost universally.

With a little practice, you'll find that these buttons are relatively easy to push. The challenge is that you may find them, as many people do, a rather unpleasant medicine. In the world of training and human resource management, it is referred to as *continuous positive praise*. My children have another name for it — "sucking up."

1. Giving Your Boss Credit

I'll never forget a conversation I had with Miles Murphy and Vince Renton in the HR department of the Technical Standards and Safety Authority. We were having an informal discussion about which individuals within their organization would be ideal candidates for heading up a potential new call center. Having recently worked with all 125 people in their head office, I said, "Well, I don't know about their work proficiency, but I can tell you from an attitude point of view I know what two people would be on my list."

"Let me see if I can guess," Miles interjected and promptly identified the two individuals I was thinking of.

Vince concurred and added a third name, to which the three of us instantly agreed.

I thought it was fascinating, and also a little reassuring,

that the same three people among such a large group stood out in our minds.

"I don't think it is a deep, dark secret within the organization," Vince went on to say, "that these individuals are shining stars."

Miles agreed. The interesting part of it was that these people were neither at a high level in the company nor in high-profile positions. They held administrative positions similar to those of many other employees. "When you think of it, it's kind of a shame," Miles added at one point, "that these people will probably never truly appreciate how much they stand out and what they bring to an organization." Sad but true.

The point is that in most companies exceptional employees stand out. Everyone knows who the contributors and the noncontributors are. Most of us have a pretty good idea what's really going on. So, when you think about it, it doesn't really matter who *takes* the credit for success in an organization — it's usually clear who truly *deserves* the credit.

If you are confident about your work, and the genuine contributions you are making to your company, it's not going to hurt you to pass on a little — or even a lot — of credit to your boss. He will appreciate the gesture, and he will appreciate you — because he believes you've made him look good. The great part of giving your boss the credit for your successes is that you lose nothing —

because most people will be able to figure out on their own where the credit really belongs.

I once got to watch a wonderfully blatant example of credit-giving while coaching in a furniture store. A salesperson, Mike, was just in the process of putting the finishing touches on a sale. He'd executed the sales process beautifully and upsold the customer from an initial $4,500 purchase to one over $8,000. As they were walking toward the sales desk to finalize the paperwork, the manager appeared. With a large smile, he walked up to the customer and said "How are we making out?" When he discovered that they had already made their purchase decision, he said "Excellent choice! You're going to love it" and then went on about his work.

After the couple had left, the boss came up to Mike and congratulated him on the sale. "Congratulations yourself!" Mike said to his boss. "It was those last few words of reinforcement you threw in that really sealed the deal." The manager walked away with a "Yeah-I-am-pretty-good-aren't-I?" grin on his face that you couldn't have peeled off with a blowtorch.

An account executive at an advertising agency I'd worked for toiled solidly for two weeks on a new business proposal. The president, after reviewing it, said, "This is excellent. Nice work!"

"Don't look at me," the account executive said modestly to the president. "I did the easy stuff. It was John here," he said, indicating his supervisor, "who really made this really come together." That account executive became John's newest favorite employee.

Giving your boss credit for work that you've done rarely costs you anything, but the payoff can be colossal. The best part is that you can be absolutely shameless about it, and your boss will never recognize what you're doing. Granted, it can be a little grating at times. Sucking up to a boss you don't like or don't respect seemingly goes against everything that is right. Some of us, in fact, find the practice of positive reinforcement with a boss so distasteful that it is simply not an option. The important thing before you discount it, I guess, is that you do a little cost-benefit analysis in your head. Yes, "sucking up" to someone might leave a bad taste in your mouth in the short term, but what are the benefits in the long term? Sometimes they can be huge.

2. Praising Your Boss
Every positive management philosophy talks about the importance of managers giving genuine positive praise and reinforcement to employees. What is rarely discussed, however, is that the same principle in reverse — employees praising their boss — works just as well. Let's face it, we all like recognition of and appreciation for our efforts. Your boss is no different. A kind word here and there can go a long way.

You don't have to make a big, grandiose gesture. Here are some types of praise that can have tremendous results.

- Hey, boss, you did a great job of organizing this project.
- I love the way you handled that customer.
- I think you made a really good decision.
- I can't get over how good you are at that!
- Nice job!

The first real job I ever had was working in a small national advertising agency in Toronto, Canada. I was a raw rookie trying very hard to earn my place in the company. For some reason, the vice-president, one of the partners in the company, didn't care for me much. He was never unkind or unfair to me, but our interactions were always somewhat cool and distant.

I was in the office early one morning talking with the office manager. It was just the two of us in the building. Out of the corner of my eye, I saw the VP come in and go into an adjoining room. He didn't know that I'd seen him. A few minutes later, on a whim, I began talking to the office manager about him. "I really admire Peter," I remember saying to her. "He's a great salesperson, and he knows so much about this industry. He's a great boss to have."

I wasn't sure he'd heard me until later that afternoon

when he came into my office. He was uncharacteristically buoyant and friendly with me. "I've been thinking that it's about time," he said, "that we start giving you a little more responsibility around here." And with that he turned one of his most prized clients over to me to manage. It was a tremendous gesture of trust on his part, and I don't think it was a coincidence.

Praising your boss, as long as it is genuine and deserved, serves two purposes: it makes him feel better about himself, and it makes him feel better about you. Both are good things and will help to make your working environment a little more enjoyable.

3. Thanking Your Boss

Here's a trick I learned many years ago from an old university friend. Every year on the anniversary of his being hired, he put a little thank-you card on his boss's desk. The first time he did it, his boss asked him what it was for. He explained that it had been a year since he was hired, and he wanted to thank him for the tremendous opportunity the boss had given him. After he told me about it, I tried it too — with tremendous success.

There are many things you can thank your boss for. Your thanks don't have to be as formal as in a thank-you card. You can simply say "Thanks for putting your trust in me," "Thanks for your help on this project," or "Thanks for your support." If your boss gives you a few hours off for personal reasons, say "Thanks for your understanding — I really appreciate it." Your boss is far more likely to treat you well when he believes that you appreciate him.

There is absolutely nothing wrong with pushing people's positive hot buttons (or, as one of my friends puts it, "gratuitous schmoozing"). You're not doing anything wrong or disingenuous, and the outcome is almost always positive. I've never heard a boss complain because an employee was too nice to him. Sure, you can go overboard. You don't want to gush. Gushing can be perceived as manipulative or false. But you'll be amazed at how thickly you can lay on the praise before someone thinks you're gushing.

Being the Model Employee

Perhaps the best way to minimize negative Boss from Hell experiences is to do your best to be a model employee. Do your job well. The better you do it, the fewer the opportunities your Boss from Hell has to practice her unique brand of torture. If other employees around you are doing the same kind of work that you are, watch them. Learn from them. Take courses, rent videos, read books. Find a reason to become passionate about the things you do and the quality of your work. If you perceive yourself as someone who's "just doing a job," with no pride in either the caliber or the value of your work, you'll never be driven to excellence. Even Bosses from Hell have a hard time finding fault with excellence.

It's also important to be loyal — both to your boss and to your company. Loyalty breeds loyalty, and a boss who becomes loyal to you is a lot easier to work with.

Most importantly, *stay positive*! By far the most common complaint I hear from bosses, good and bad alike, is about employees who are negative: negative about their jobs, their coworkers, their bosses, their personal lives. And by far the most common lame excuse that negative employees use is "It's not my fault I'm negative — it's my boss/job/wife/husband/etc." Attitude, as I've mentioned before, is completely under your control, and there is no excuse for having a negative one. Make it your mission to become the happiest darned employee your boss has ever seen. You'll be astounded at the results.

Finally, make an effort to go above and beyond the call of duty. If your shift ends at 9:00, stay until 9:10 if you still have a bit of work to do. Bring forward ideas and suggestions. Look for better, faster, more efficient ways of doing things. Demonstrate to your boss that you are genuinely interested in his success and the success of the business.

Setting Your Own Goals

My wife has this wonderful technique she uses whenever she has to do something painful or unpleasant — going to the dentist, having surgery, that sort of thing. She doesn't use anesthetic. Instead, she's developed the ability to take her thoughts off the pain and retreat to a very pleasant corner of her mind. She calls it her "happy place."

She taught her technique to me, and I was surprised at how well it works. I was trying to take up a regimen of running every day. I loved the exercise, but my biggest challenge was the boredom. After 15 minutes, I would find it tedious to the point of agony. More often than not, I would quit my run, not because I was tired but because I was bored. The results of finding my own happy place while running have been wonderful. As I begin running, I let my mind drift to my own little happy place. Before I know it, 30 minutes have passed.

You can accomplish the same thing in an unpleasant working environment. Not, of course, by letting your mind wander, but by using some simple techniques to create a little island of comfort in the sea of unpleasantness surrounding you. It all begins by clearly defining what it is you really want out of your job and setting goals for yourself. It's not really that hard, but it does require a shift in the way you look at things.

Most of us are content to simply show up for work

and deal with whatever happens when we get there. We do what we're told, and we hope that the boss is going to make our work satisfying. We let our environment tell us what to expect from work instead of finding out for ourselves what we want from work. What you really need to identify, given your current working environment and your Boss from Hell, are goals that will help to motivate you throughout the day and allow you to go to bed at night satisfied that it was a good day.

Start by taking a close look at what you do for a living. What parts of your job do you enjoy? What are the things you do that bring you satisfaction? What value do you bring to the company? What would happen to the company if your position ceased to exist? What can you personally take pride in that your boss can't take away from you?

I once met a young woman, Barbara, who worked full time in the customer service center of a large, super-regional mall. She was delightful. Her positive attitude and effervescent personality were instantly apparent to everyone who met her. Barbara was among the 10 full-time and part-time employees who worked there.

The employees not only looked after customers in the mall but also ran the telephone switchboard for the mall administration office. And when I called to speak with the mall manager or marketing director, it was almost always Barbara's voice I heard first. It was a great way to begin a telephone call. Barbara was always cheery and upbeat.

The center supervisor, according to the others, was the Boss from Hell. She was cold and condescending, and her staff considered her grossly unfair when it came to setting shifts or giving them time off. She was continually taking credit for everyone else's performance and publicly berating employees when they made mistakes. Her behavior drove the other employees to distraction, and the turnover rate in the center was exceedingly high. How she ever became a supervisor in a customer service center is beyond me.

The only person seemingly unaffected by her behavior was Barbara. At one point, I asked her why this was. "Well, there's no question she has issues," Barbara said, "and she's not a terribly pleasant person to be around. But I can't let her get to me. I take a lot of pride in what I do, and, if I focus too much on her bizarre behavior, I'll lose my focus on the customers. And if I'm not giving good service to my customers, what's the point of me even being here?"

Barbara's happy place was happy customers. The happier they were, the happier she was. Barbara was able to ignore her manager's odd behavior and thus not let it stand in the way of her doing a good job.

She explained to me that it hadn't always been that way. When the manager first started, Barbara, too, became distraught at her behavior. When she became aware of the negative effect it was having on her life, she made a conscious decision to ignore it and focus on her work — with tremendous results.

The first question you need to ask yourself is "What do I want to get out of work?" What brings you job satisfaction? Maybe it's creating new relationships. If you're in the customer service business, like Barbara, maybe it's happy customers. If you're an engineer or a computer programmer, maybe it's solving problems or coming up with new and better ways of doing things. If you're a trainer, maybe it's when you've enhanced people's skill sets or made some other difference in their lives. One thing is certain: if you're working just for the money, and that's the only thing you ever hope to get out of your job, your boss is the least of your problems. Given that we spend about half of our available hours at work, money itself just isn't enough.

Once you've identified what brings you pride in your work, the next step is to determine how you can achieve it on a continuing, daily basis. The nice thing about having pride in your work is that nobody can ever take it away from you — not even the Boss from Hell. It raises your self-esteem and helps you to put other things in perspective.

Another important part of creating your happy place at work is a focus on building your support network. Get to know the people you work with — *all* the people you work with. Help them out whenever you have an opportunity. Work with them. Back them up. Support them. Your workplace satisfaction will grow significantly as your support network grows. The fact is it's a lot easier to look out for number one when you have a bunch of other people looking out for you as well.

Finally, try hard to maintain your perspective. Don't let the stress of your job, or your Boss from Hell, make you lose sight of what is really important. If your Boss from Hell is really starting to push your buttons, try to remember why you are working in the first place. You have friends, family, and outside activities that bring you enjoyment. Often, focusing on those positive aspects of our lives can make some of the negative things a little more palatable.

And, despite what your Boss from Hell might tell you, don't forget how good you are and the contributions you bring to the company. Make a list of your strengths. Keep them somewhere handy. Remember that people have been hiring you for a reason, and, unless you're a supermodel, it probably hasn't just been for your good looks.

CHAPTER FOUR

COVERING YOUR BUTT 101

Remember the motto of the Boy Scout: "Be Prepared."

There's an old saying in football: "The best defense is a good offense." It's based on the theory that, if you can keep the other team on the defensive for the whole game, they'll never have an opportunity to score a goal on you. The same principle is true in a work environment with a Boss from Hell. You don't actually want to put your boss on the defensive, of course. We discussed earlier why that is a Bad Idea. But you can make it uncomfortable or difficult for him to choose you as a target. You achieve this with tried-and-true BCTS (Butt-Covering Techniques).

In the fast-paced, high-stress world of advertising agencies, BCTS are common. Doug, a print production manager I once worked with, was a master at it. I remember the first time I had to work with him.

I walked into his office with a project in my hand and said, "Can you have this ready by the end of the month?"

He said he could, but asked me to give him a note confirming when I wanted it. "Otherwise, I'll forget," he told me.

On the 24th of the month, I walked into his office and asked where the job was. "The client is screaming for it," I said with a little exaggeration.

"Then you should have asked to have it completed by today," he responded calmly.

"I did!" I shot back. "And you said it would be ready!"

Doug calmly walked over to a bunch of file folders on his desk, opened one, and pulled out the note I'd given him asking for the job at the end of the month. "Near as I can tell," he said with a slight grin, "I've still got close to a whole week left."

There wasn't much I could say, of course. I cringed at the thought of having to call my client to tell her that she still had another week to wait.

As I was walking out of his office, Doug said to me, "I didn't say I didn't have it done, you know." When I turned back to look at him, he was pointing to a cardboard box in the corner of his office. His grin was so big I thought the corners of his lips would meet at the back of his head and the top of his head would fall off.

Doug's message came across loud and clear: "I'll do my best to deliver when promised, but don't mess with me!" Over the years I spent at that agency, I watched Doug train a lot of people in the same way he trained me. He kept his butt covered, and I can honestly say I never saw anyone mess with him twice.

His method of covering his butt was ensuring that all instructions to him were made in writing. And as long as Doug lived up to his end of the bargain, the people whom he worked for had no choice but to leave him alone. There are other BCTs that work equally well.

Keep Stuff

Keep copies of all correspondence that you either send or receive. If possible, try to keep hard copies. Computers have a way of crashing at inopportune moments. Stuff has a way of coming in handy, particularly if you have a manipulative or ethically challenged boss. A friend of mine has boxes of stuff he's accumulated over the past six years. He refers to them as his "insurance policies."

Keep Journals

I know a couple of people who are big believers in keeping daily work journals. They don't put anything personal in them, of course, but they make a point of recording their activities during the day. They leave them out on their desks so that everyone knows they are there and use them to refer back to things that may be in dispute. A Boss from Hell will think twice before he says or does something that might be recorded or contradicts something already recorded.

Make cc's and bcc's

This is the original BCT classic. Whenever you have to correspond with the Boss from Hell, make sure that someone else is either copied (cc'd) or blind-copied (bcc'd). The cc will be visible to your boss and might raise questions in his mind about why you're making one, so be sure you have a logical explanation ready. The bcc will raise questions in the recipient's mind, so make sure that she is aware of why you are copying her. Remember that the purpose of a cc or bcc is to inform a relevant, interested third party of your activity. So make sure that it is a logical and appropriate thing to do. If it doesn't appear logical or appropriate, your Boss from Hell might think you are doing it for some other purpose, and it could create even more challenges for you.

Confirmation and Information

E-mail is proving to be a terrific tool for butt-covering. It's fast, it's a little less formal than an interoffice memo, and people get so many of them that they often don't pay a lot of attention to certain types. Quick, one- or two-sentence e-mails are all you need to create a permanent record of who said what to whom. There are two reasons (excuses) for sending them: confirmation and information.

Confirmation

A confirming e-mail should be informal, brief, and breezy. The less it looks like an official confirmation, the less uncomfortable it will make your Boss from Hell. Here are a couple of examples of formal and informal ways to write a confirmation e-mail.

Formal confirmation

John:

This is to confirm our conversation today and our understanding that you will be making the arrangements for all of the personnel logistics and that I will be responsible for the operational aspects of the project. . . .

Informal confirmation

Hi John:

Since you're looking after the personnel, and I'm looking after the operations, will you be needing any of the files I have?

Formal confirmation

Susan:

I just wanted to confirm what my responsibilities will be on the project we discussed today. I am to interface with our design team and co-ordinate the development. . . .

Informal confirmation

Hi Susan:

Just a quick question – on this project, where I'm interfacing with the design team and coordinating the development – which should take priority?

In each pair, identical information is conveyed in the formal and informal e-mails. The key difference between the formal and informal styles is that in the formal style the confirmation is presented as the primary purpose of the e-mail, while in the informal style the confirmation is simply incidental to an information request. The first raises red flags for your boss that you are trying to get things in writing. The second achieves the same goal while positioning your action as simply trying to be helpful.

Information

An FYI e-mail is a terrific way to document Boss from Hell activities and other things you'd like to record. As with the confirmation e-mail, an information e-mail should be brief, to the point, and indirect (focused on something other than butt-covering).

Hi Boss:

Just to give you an update on the project. I've focused on the inventory count, as you suggested. It's done — along with the merchandising plan-o-gram. Ran out of time on the training program.

Bobby

In this example, Bobby has preempted any opportunity the boss may have had to get angry over Bobby's not getting around to the training program. It was, after all, the boss who set the priorities. Bobby has also created some documentation to protect himself if his actions are ever questioned by someone else.

Find a Champion

If your organization has a hierarchy, such as a senior management team, make an effort to build bonds with one or more of that group. You don't have to become best buddies with someone; you just have to build a positive relationship. Volunteer for committees that a senior company member is involved with. Help out with projects. Make it a point to let someone above your boss know that you are interested in the well-being of the company.

It may take some time, but once you have a positive, respectful working relationship with someone who is superior to your boss you'll begin to notice changes in how your boss approaches you. He too will become more respectful. He won't be quite sure how deep your relationship is and will be careful how he treats you.

Your champion can also become a mentor when things get difficult. Although it is rarely a good idea to go over your boss's head, it can be tremendously valuable to have someone to turn to for guidance and advice. If you happen to have a Boss from Hell standing between you and a promotion, your champion can help to open doors previously closed to you.

Covering your butt is a basic tactic even if you don't have a Boss from Hell. You never know when your situation might change, and a butt-covering technique can save you a lot of grief. You don't have to become paranoid, of course; just remember the motto of the Boy Scout: "Be Prepared."

PART TWO

HELL IN A HANDBASKET

Always before him many of them stand;
They go by turns each one unto the judgment;
They speak, and hear, and then are downward
hurled.

— Dante's *Inferno*

CHAPTER FIVE

YOUR FIRST LINE OF DEFENSE

> When you choose not to take action,
> you are also choosing to leave your
> destiny in the hands of others.

Nothing, as they say, lasts forever. Dynasties crumble, walls come down, things change. A scant 30 years ago, retail giants such as Woolworth's and Kmart were thought to be unstoppable. Little did anyone suspect that an enterprising individual by the name of Sam Walton would come along and redefine the retail landscape with his Wal-Mart stores. Seemingly unassailable icons such as Polaroid, IBM, Nortel, and Xerox became embattled. Social and cultural standards in the world changed with the dissolution of the Soviet Union, the reintegration of Germany, the fall of apartheid, the end of slavery, etc.

All of these things, in their time, were considered the norm. And the people living in those times and places couldn't envision life any other way. We're no different today. We have a hard time bringing ourselves to imagine a world different than the one we live in at the moment. But the timeless truth is that change is the only thing we can truly count on. Change is a part of every element of our lives. People change, companies change, and bosses change.

A friend of mine works for the post office in its head office. "I've had six bosses in the last ten years," he once said to me. "When someone new comes along that I don't like, I just wait them out and hope the next one will be better." I've heard dozens of stories of people finally quitting their job out of frustration with their boss only to find out three months later that the boss quit to work elsewhere. You never know when your boss is going to quit, be fired, be transferred, retire, or even, unfortunately, be promoted. Sometimes the best plan is to treat your Boss from Hell like a tornado, where all you really need to do is find yourself a safe place and wait him out.

In the next five chapters, I will outline your FIRST line of defense — five things you can do to make living with your boss a little easier while you wait him out. Sometimes you can change him. Sometimes he'll leave. Sometimes, unfortunately, neither of those things happens — but it's at least worth a shot.

The FIRST line of defense is

Fly below the radar;
Ignore;
Retrain;
Stand your ground; and
Talk turkey.

FIRST is a series of strategies to help you gain more control over your life at work. Learning to control your own destiny is a critical concept, not only in helping you better deal with your Boss from Hell, but also in helping you manage difficult situations in the workplace and in your personal life.

One of the most common mistakes we make is that we all too easily surrender control of our lives. In a very real sense, we give away our power. We don't do it on purpose, of course. In fact, most people are completely unaware of what's really happening. The only thing we recognize is the powerless, helpless feeling that comes as a result. Having power or control over our lives means making our own choices and not letting others make them for us.

Whenever we relinquish our power to choose, we give away our control. And we relinquish our power to choose every time we find someone or something to blame things on. Life is about choices. We choose our companions. We choose what we eat. We choose where we work. We choose what we do for recreation. But too often we take the easy way out by convincing ourselves that those choices don't exist. And every time we do that, we tell the world that we are powerless.

We say things such as "I'm trapped in my job" when nothing could be further from the truth. Unless you're physically chained to your desk, or working in the prison license plate factory, the fact is you simply haven't chosen to seek employment elsewhere. We trap ourselves, and the bars that keep us captive are our fears. Our fears of change, of failure, of the unknown. Here are some other common statements you might hear around the workplace.

- My boss is making me work late again.
- I have to get this done.
- This job is killing me.
- My workload is huge.

In each example, it seems as though there's no other option. The Horrible Things happening to us seem to be completely beyond our control. Consider, though, how the nature of the statements changes when they are presented as choices.

- I've decided to work late again.
- I want to get this done.
- I am letting this job kill me.
- I've taken on a huge workload.

The issues are the same, but the difference in the statements is profound. In the second set of examples, we have acknowledged that the decisions to do these things were ours — not someone else's. The first set of examples positions us as victims.

The victim mentality is endemic in today's society. Few of us, it seems, want to be held accountable for our own actions. We wait for other people to solve our problems and avoid looking within ourselves for solutions. The victim mentality drains us of our self-confidence and our willingness to be proactive. Acknowledging our choices, on the other hand, forces us down a path of self-determination.

Let's take the second set of examples again and examine their repercussions.

"I've decided to work late again." Once you've said this, the first question that springs to mind is "Why?" Why have you decided to work late again? That question is quickly followed by a flurry of others. "Is there something I'd rather be doing?" "Is this really more important than those other things?" "If so, why did I choose to do this?" All of the questions scream for answers, and it is those answers that can help you to identify more rewarding courses of action.

Let's say that your answer to the question "Why have I decided to work late again?" is "Because, if I don't, I might get fired!" This statement creates a whole new set of questions, not the least of which are "Would changing jobs really be such a bad thing?" and "Is this job really so important to me that I'm willing to sacrifice my family or friends?" If the answers to both of those questions are "No," then you've begun empowering yourself, giving yourself the confidence to make some difficult decisions.

"I want to get this done." Again the question is "Why?" Maybe your answer is that you take a lot of pride in your work and don't like loose ends. Again you've empowered yourself. You're no longer taking action because of some negative, uncontrollable influence; you're now taking it because of a positive belief in your own set of high standards. Now, when you go home, instead of feeling like a helpless victim of your work, you feel proud of your work ethic.

"I'm letting this job kill me." "Why?" Is it because you are hoping for a promotion? A raise perhaps? If so, then you might want to examine how realistic those goals are. Ask yourself how important they really are to you and whether or not they're worth the current pain. If you decide that "Yes, the stress I'm going through right now will be worth the payoff," then you have something positive to look forward to. The pain becomes less of an issue as you weigh it against the future benefits.

"I've taken on a huge workload." Again your answer to "Why?" will lead you in an empowering direction. Maybe your answer is "Because I thought I could handle it." The next question becomes "Can I really?" If the answer is "No," then you might begin to think of ways to reduce the workload you are currently under.

The empowering approach forces you to ask yourself why you are doing things. It places the responsibility for your actions squarely on your shoulders, and you begin to realize that you have the power to change things if you wish. This approach helps you to take control over your situation and your destiny and gives you confidence in your decisions.

Of course, the victim approach also gets you asking "Why?" questions. But far from being empowering, these questions will simply make you feel more powerless. "Why do they always do these things to me?" "Why am I always the one to work late?" "Why is my boss so insensitive to my needs?" "Why can't they give this work to someone else?"

The more you begin to realize how much power you actually have, the more comfortable you become with yourself and those around you. Bosses from Hell become less of an issue because you're aware of how little they can really do to you. Your destiny becomes more your own, and you begin finding your work environment a lot more enjoyable.

Accepting your power requires courage, however. You see, it's not enough to just accept the premise that you are in the driver's seat. Knowing that it is you who are controlling things, and that they aren't just randomly happening to you, is only the first part of the equation. The second part is accepting that you are also choosing the *consequences* of your actions. Whether you like it or not, when you choose to work late, you also choose to ignore your family. When you choose to take on a lot of work, you also choose to accept the stress. Just as you can't choose to smoke without the risk of getting cancer, and can't choose to eat ice cream without the risk of getting fat, so too you can't choose to do what you're doing without also taking the blame for the consequences.

Before you can really begin to deal with your Boss from Hell, you have to accept that you have complete control over the things you do. You have to recognize that you don't *have* to do anything and that you are instead *choosing* to do things. If you don't believe you have the power to change things, how will you ever have the power to deal with your boss?

FIRST comprises five things that you can control when working with your Boss from Hell. These are five strategies that can, at the very least, make going into work a little more tolerable. You may choose, of course, not to try them. But always remember that, when you choose not to take action, you are also choosing to leave your destiny in the hands of others.

CHAPTER SIX

FLY BELOW THE RADAR

Like the chameleon, you want to blend into the surroundings so that the potential predators in the area don't notice you.

Back in the olden days before satellites and GPS, militaries relied exclusively on radar to detect incoming aircraft. For a plane to approach a destination without being detected, the pilot had to fly at extremely low levels so that radar stations couldn't see it through the Earth's horizon. It was referred to as "flying below the radar."

A similar technique is effective when dealing with a Boss from Hell. The principle is that, when he is looking for someone to blame, someone to dump on, or someone to irritate, he can't pick on people he can't see. There are a number of different ways to fly below a boss's radar. Their effectiveness depends, of course, on the type of Boss from Hell you have, but you should find that at least one of these ways will reduce the amount of bad behavior directed at you.

1. Create No Threat

As we discussed earlier, the fastest way to create challenges with your Boss from Hell is to make him feel threatened in some way. Like cornering a wild animal, threatening your boss leaves you wide open for attack. At the very least, direct or indirect threats are guaranteed CLMs. Not only do you want to avoid making specific threats against him, but you also don't want him to perceive you to be a threat in general.

While I was working on a project with a large high-tech firm, a vice-president gave me the lowdown on one of his managers. "He's pretty good," he said. "He knows his stuff and has progressed quite quickly up the ranks. As I've mentioned to the president, though, I think he may be moving a little too quickly. I think he should stay where he is for a while, just so he can become a little more seasoned. I've just moved him off one of the more high-profile projects so that he can get a little experience in some other areas."

The manager in question was, frankly, more than capable of completing the original project. And the projects he'd been transferred to were similar to ones he'd worked on two years previously. I had difficulty following the VP's logic. Talking with other people, though, I discovered that this was a common practice with this vp and that most people in the manager's position eventually left the company to pursue opportunities elsewhere.

The vp's decision to transfer the manager from the project had far less to do, it seems, with "seasoning" him than it did with removing a threat to his own position. The next rung in the corporate ladder for this manager's position, it turned out, was vp. The manager, simply by doing his job well, had made himself a perceived threat to an insecure boss.

Even if you aren't a threat to your boss's position, he may still perceive you as a threat to his authority. A manipulator, in discovering that he can't control you as easily as he does others, might become concerned that your coworkers will begin to follow your example. If you happen to have a great deal of subject matter expertise, and people come directly to you for answers, a boss might feel that you are replacing him in some way. If customers regularly ask to deal with you specifically, he might think he is considered second best.

So the question is how can you keep doing a great job in such a way that your boss doesn't perceive you as a threat? I hate to say it, but it all boils back down to that sucking-up thing again.

If you're in a situation where your boss feels threatened by you, the best way to make him feel a little more comfortable is by constantly reminding him that you haven't lost sight of who's really the boss. A look into the military gives us some clues about how this approach can work. A sergeant training new recruits, for example, has absolute authority in his work. He calls all the shots and makes all the decisions. In fulfilling that role, he must be strong and unequivocal, and he must not defer to anyone. When talking with the CO (commanding officer), however, the same hard-nosed authority figure becomes unconditionally deferential. He salutes. He stands only when the CO stands. He speaks only when spoken to. He takes direction without question — even if he believes it to be wrong. This rigid command-and-control military regimen works exceedingly well and has a number of significant benefits. First, it facilitates rapid and efficient action because no time is wasted in debate. Second, it enables the military to execute multi-team maneuvers with precision — the leaders confident that their subordinates won't begin to take individual action. Third, and not the least important, senior officers aren't in the position where they constantly have to look over their shoulders, worried about the intentions or motivations of those who report to them. When conflict does arise in military organizations, it is frequently a result of a subordinate's questioning a superior's judgment or decision.

The television series *The West Wing* gives us another example of deferential behavior. In the show, Jed Bartlet (played by Martin Sheen) is the president of the United States, and Leo McGarry (played by John Spencer) is his best friend and chief of staff. Despite their longtime friendship, however, McGarry refers to Bartlet as "Mr. President" — even when they are in private. In doing so, he continually sends the message "You're the boss."

Although our jobs may not be quite as strict or formal as those of a military hierarchy or White House protocol, there are some behavioral lessons we can learn. You don't have to start saluting, of course, but you can do a number of little things to send that message of deference and respect to your boss.

- When he speaks, nod your head in agreement. Don't overdo it, of course (you don't want to come across as one of those little bobble-head dogs that sit in the back window of a car), but use a quick, silent nod of affirmation.

- When you've had a success, use the word *we* instead of *I*. For example, "We just closed another sale!" "It looks like we're going to come in under budget!" "I think we've got this one figured out."

- Make sure that you clearly convey your respect for the things your boss does well. Let him know that he is, in some way, a role model for you.

- Ask your boss for his advice, input, or opinion whenever you have the opportunity. You'll communicate to him that you value his knowledge and skill.

- Here's a big one: practice saying "Yes" instead of "Yabut." Yabut or "Yes, but . . ." is a phrase we often use when our opinion differs from that of our boss. "Yabut we've tried that before." "Yabut it's the wrong time of year." "Yabut I had to do that last time." As far as your boss is concerned, any yabut is a challenge. It is simply another way of saying "I disagree." A good alternative to saying "Yes, but . . ." is simply "Yes." You can even try "Yes, and. . . ." Yabut is a guaranteed way to raise your head above that radar.

- Finally, try to put everything in his terms. To the best of your ability, make things sound as though they were his idea — or at least as though it was his idea that triggered your idea. For example, instead of saying "Hey, boss, I think we should start using Ship-Fast instead of that courier company we're using now," you can say "Hey, boss, remember how you were talking about wanting to improve that delivery system? I was thinking it might be worthwhile trying ShipFast to see if it would help." Here's another example. Instead of saying "Hey, boss, we're going to need some training if we're going to reduce the number of escalated complaints," you can say "Hey, boss, I think you're right that we should be able to reduce the number of customer complaints that get escalated to you. Do you think some training might help?"

2. Keep Your Opinions to Yourself

Opinions are like noses — everyone has one (and some of them really smell!). If you want to fly below your Boss from Hell's radar, however, you have to wrap your head around the idea that her opinion is the only one that's important. One surefire way to draw attention to yourself is to publicly disagree with her. If your boss expresses an opinion about a thing, person, or project, your best bet is just to nod and keep your mouth shut. You don't actually have to endorse her point of view, but you certainly don't want to challenge it. If she asks you for your opinion, make it clear, regardless of what you think, it's what she thinks that really counts. Here's an example.

> **Boss:** Susan, I think that Richard down at Accounting has either got to be the stupidest human being on the planet or else he's out to get us and doing this on purpose. Personally, I think he's doing these things on purpose. I mean, how else do you explain it? What do you think?
>
> **Susan:** (who likes Richard in Accounting) I agree; it sure looks that way. But I don't understand – he seems like such a nice guy. I wonder if he's just overworked or something.

Susan acknowledged the validity of her boss's point of view while at the same time getting her point of view across. She stayed true to her conviction without raising any red flags with her boss. Had she said, for example, "Naw, he's not out to get you. He's just overworked," she would have directly contradicted her boss and sent the message to him that she's not someone he can turn to for support.

3. Don't Take Sides

Your boss and a coworker — Charlie — get into a fight. Charlie is upset because your boss didn't support him when a customer came in to complain. The boss, fuming, comes to you and says "I can't believe that Charlie is angry! Because I looked after a customer? What was I supposed to do? Tell the customer that she was stupid and to just go away? That guy's got to get control of his ego, don't you agree?"

You're now in that awkward position of having to say something negative about a coworker or having to defend him to your boss. Whichever side you choose, you lose. Even if you sit on the fence, your boss might perceive that as disagreement. The best strategy is to say something that reaffirms your respect for your boss. For example, you might want to say "I don't envy you being put in that position!" or "I'm glad I don't have your job!" Both reaffirm your respect for his position without making a comment on his actual decision.

4. Try to Be a Team Player

There is nothing more frustrating for a boss than when one of his team isn't pulling her weight or playing nicely with the rest of the team. If the team isn't functioning well together, and the boss perceives that you might be the root cause of the problem, his radar will automatically perk up. What this means is that you have to make a concerted effort to get along with your coworkers. Yes, sometimes you find yourself sitting next to the Coworker from Hell, who may be exceedingly difficult to get along with. But the bottom line is that you don't want your manager to believe that *you* are the problem. Here are the five things you have to do to be a good team player.

1. *Open lines of communication.* Make sure your team members are always aware of what you're doing and why you're doing it. Make sure that you are open to their communication – answer their e-mails, return their phone calls, etc.

2. *Treat coworkers with respect.* Acknowledge their ideas and input and never lose sight of common courtesy. If you have a disagreement with a coworker, focus on resolving it instead of winning it.

3. *Trust coworkers.* Trust people to do the jobs they are charged to do. Recognize and respect that they may work at a different tempo or have a different work style from you. Don't try to take over their work, or tell them how to do their jobs, or give them any unsolicited advice. If, for some reason, they are unable to do their part, just be supportive and offer any help you can.

4. *Focus on the team's goal.* Don't get distracted by other things. Remember that, just as you are relying on your team members, they too are relying on you.

5. *Take action*. When action needs to be taken, don't procrastinate. Always be an active and positive participant on your team.

5. Don't Spring Surprises

Communication, or lack of communication, can play a huge role in whether or not you hit your boss's radar screen. It's a delicate balance. On the one hand, flying below the radar means keeping as quiet as possible when it comes to opinions and arguments. On the other hand, when it comes to your day-to-day business, the rule is the more communication the better. Failure to communicate with your boss in an accurate and timely manner can create the perception that you're trying to keep her out of the loop. This failure can also have serious consequences if the information you didn't share with your boss turns out to be significant.

An assembly line worker in an automobile plant once failed to tell a boss about a slight vibration that had begun in some of the equipment he was using. A few days later that equipment seized up as the nut, which had come loose, fell into the gear assembly — ruining the whole mechanism. Not only was his workstation closed, but the entire assembly line was also shut down for almost a week before they got the equipment fixed. The manager was understandably furious when the employee told him afterward that he'd suspected there might be a problem.

As a rule, bosses don't like surprises. They particularly don't like it when they are seemingly the only ones who are surprised. Make sure you tell your boss everything that's going on — and don't avoid the unpleasant stuff. Often we avoid telling our boss these things because we are concerned about how she will respond. Chances are, though, she will respond a lot better to problems when she is the first, rather than the last, to know about them.

One thing to be careful of — as you make it a practice to keep your boss informed, try not to come across as a bad-news maven. If your boss perceives you as someone who spends all your time pointing out problems, she may begin to think of you as negative and as a draining influence on the team — the exact opposite of the image you're trying to achieve.

Flying below the radar means trying to be as invisible as possible. Like the chameleon, you want to blend into the surroundings so that the potential predators in the area don't notice you. You are not a threat, you are not a concern, you are not a hindrance to anyone achieving his goal. In your Boss from Hell's world, you are just this innocent little cog in her machine, whirring soundlessly and effortlessly and certainly not worth her attention.

CHAPTER SEVEN

IGNORE

Sometimes the best response is no response.

We discussed earlier how we can sometimes be guilty of unwittingly triggering bad behavior in our bosses with the things we do and say. In those unfortunate situations, our priority becomes how to avoid doing anything that might escalate that behavior. We want to prevent things from going from bad to worse. And, to accomplish this, sometimes the best response is no response. Unless your boss's behavior affects you in some negative way, your best bet is simply to try to ignore it. If retreating into your Happy Place isn't working for some reason, here are a few things to try.

Do a Cost-Benefit Analysis

There's an age-old saying that "You have to choose your battles." And nowhere is it truer than with the Boss from Hell. Let's face it — it's to no one's benefit if you work yourself into the frantic dithers every time your boss does something stupid. You're better off focusing only on those things that have a direct and significant impact on your life and ignoring the rest. Chances are, if you do a simple cost-benefit exercise on what you should and shouldn't do, you'll discover that the best bet in the majority of cases is just to ignore him. There are two key questions to ask when deciding whether your boss's action is worth ignoring or pursuing.

Is It Impacting You Personally?

Is his action impacting you directly? If what he is doing is just an annoyance, or if his behavior is impacting a coworker or the company, ignore it. Sure, if your coworker is looking for some support, you may want to become involved, but otherwise stay out of it. As they say in prison, you do your own time.

Not helping a coworker in need can be difficult, particularly if you happen to be very compassionate or if you are easily outraged by unfairness and injustice in general. The question you have to ask yourself, though, is what the cost is of becoming involved, emotionally or otherwise, in something that doesn't impact you directly. For starters, there's the emotional cost. Your stress level goes up — and who needs more of that? There's also the real possibility that becoming involved could trigger even more bad boss behavior — this time directed at you. Is there a benefit to becoming involved?

That's a tough question, and the answer depends on the situation. But you really have to look at it carefully. If you're having a hard time identifying a personal benefit to your action, chances are there is no benefit at all.

Is It Important?

I once had a boss who referred to employees who worked for him by their last names — Mr. Belding, Ms. Smith, and so on. He came across as pretentious and condescending, but most of us just ignored it, thinking of it as a minor irritation at worst. It made one of my coworkers nuts, however, and she finally blurted out an angry "My name is *Julie!*"

Suddenly, Julie began to command an awful lot more unpleasant Boss from Hell attention. Now, whenever he acknowledged her, he called her *Julie*. If we were in a group, he made a point of saying "Hello, Mr. Belding, hello, Ms. Smith, hello . . . *Julie.*" His continued emphasis on using her first name drove her to near distraction.

Why did Julie choose to fight this particular battle with the boss? She felt that she was being treated disrespectfully. What she failed to consider was that, with a public confrontation, she might make matters worse. In retrospect, and given the outcome, Julie would likely agree that our boss's using our last names probably wasn't worth getting all worked up about.

Think Long Term

With any action you take, there can be both short-term and long-term benefits. And often the two are quite different. For example, if you pay all of your bills on time, the short-term benefit is that you don't have to worry about making interest payments or having creditors chasing you. The long-term benefit is that you develop a solid, positive credit rating that allows you to get mortgages, car loans, etc.

When we're thinking of reacting to a Boss from Hell's behavior, it's a focus on the perceived short-term benefits that usually gets us in trouble. For instance, making a sarcastic remark to your boss may have the short-term benefit of bringing you a little instant gratification. But in the long run, you're likely to have a lot more pain than gain. Julie's decision to confront our Boss from Hell gave her the short-term satisfaction that she had stood her ground and put him in his place. In the long term, however, all she got was more grief.

Learn to Reframe

Reframing is a wonderful technique that allows you to put your boss's actions into a context that you can live with. While you may not agree with him, and you may still dislike him, it does make it a little easier to ignore the things he does. Reframing, in its simplest terms, is the process of learning to look at things from a different perspective. It is redefining the motivation for someone's actions into something a little more positive and a lot more palatable.

Let's say, for example, that you have a boss who makes it a regular practice of belittling the people around him. "This guy is an arrogant jerk" you may think to yourself. While your assessment may be accurate, it is a perspective that works against you. Let's face it, it's very hard to ignore an arrogant jerk. Think about how your feelings might change, however, if you were to reframe it like this: "That guy must really have low self-esteem to feel the need to always put everybody down." Same boss, same action — but ascribing a different motivation to his action changes it a little. You now see his action as stemming from a weakness — low self-esteem — as opposed to the potentially stronger position of a sense of superiority. It's a bit easier to ignore someone's actions when you feel sorry for that person.

Here are some other examples of reframing.

For an Indecisive Boss
Original thought: This guy is wishy-washy.
Reframed: He doesn't like to make a decision unless
    he's absolutely positive.

For a Boss Who Often Explodes and Goes on Rants
Original thought: This guy is crazy.
Reframed: This guy is very passionate.

For a Boss Who Is Cold and Abrupt
Original thought: This guy is miserable.
Reframed: This guy doesn't have a lot of
    interpersonal skills.

In each of these examples, both the original thought and the reframed thought are equally valid. The reframed thought, however, puts you in a stronger position, which in turn will reduce your level of frustration. To reframe behavior effectively, you have to be willing to step back for a moment and examine the situation, not from the viewpoint of the impact the Boss from Hell is having on you but from the perspective of why he's doing the things he's doing. As we discussed in the first chapter, a multitude of factors can contribute to a Boss from Hell's behavior. A close examination of them gives you the perspective required for effective reframing.

Create a Safe Environment

I'm on the road close to 200 days of the year with speaking engagements, training sessions, meetings, and so on. It can sometimes be draining, and dragging luggage from hotel to hotel can really become tedious. Many years back, however, I began to make a practice of carrying with me at all times pictures of my family, which I always unpack first and put on the bedside table. That way I'm always reminded of why I'm on the road in the first place. They also serve as a reminder to me that, whatever else may happen to me, I always have people in my life who care about me.

Whether you work in an office, in a cubicle, at a workstation, or behind a store counter, try to mold it into a space that brings you comfort. It could be photographs of family or friends, plants for the room, plaques or certificates commemorating your achievements, or something as simple as your favorite cartoon taped to your computer monitor. One young woman I know who works in a gift store brings to work every morning a freshly cut flower. She claims that it helps to keep her happy.

Just like a kid playing hide and seek, you're trying to build a "home base." Some safe place where you can always go back to. Something that helps you to put the world in a better perspective. The more enjoyable your environment is, the less stress you feel. And the less stress you feel, the easier it becomes to ignore the silly things that happen around you.

Learning how to ignore your boss's behavior (without, of course, ignoring his instructions) can be a very valuable tool for helping you tolerate him on a daily basis. It won't make him behave any better, and it won't make him any more likable, but it will help you to get through the day. Hopefully, if you can survive enough days, things will change for the better.

CHAPTER EIGHT

RETRAIN

Like it or not, we humans aren't that different
from dogs when it comes to motivation.

I once had a secretary named Franca. She was an absolutely wonderful person and a delight to work with. I'll never forget our introduction. She looked at me squarely with a little twinkle in her eye and said "Well, now, how long do you suppose it's going to take to train you?" We all laughed at the time, but six months later I realized that she had not only trained me but trained me well.

Since that time, I've watched many people train their bosses with tremendous results, and I've had the chance to talk with a number of them to find out how they do it. I learned that there are five techniques for training your boss to be a nicer person.

Positive and Negative Reinforcement

One thing that we all have in common, your Boss from Hell included, is that our motivation really revolves around only two things: pain and pleasure. People take action (or avoid taking action) either on things that will bring them pleasure or on things that will help them avoid pain. You go to work every morning to gain the pleasure of the paycheck and to avoid the pain that comes from having no money. We drink coffee because it's pleasant. We don't gulp it because we might burn ourselves. We don't ask the cute girl to the dance to avoid the pain of rejection, while somebody else more motivated by the pleasure of her company does.

Have you ever trained a dog? In one hand you have a rolled-up newspaper and in the other a doggie biscuit. Well, like it or not, we humans aren't that different from dogs when it comes to motivation. And it's the simple and subtle use of the same pain-and-pleasure principle that works in training your Boss from Hell. The basics are that, when she's behaving well, you respond positively, and when she's behaving badly you respond either neutrally or slightly negatively.

For example, when your boss turns to you and asks you nicely "Hey, will you do this for me please?" respond with a big smile and jump right to it. When your boss doesn't ask you so nicely, acknowledge her with a

somber nod and tell her you'll get right to it as soon as
you're finished what you're working on. You'll be
amazed at how quickly you will begin to see results from
this little exercise in behavioral modification — as long
as you're consistent in reinforcing the positive behavior
and discouraging the negative behavior.

To retrain effectively, it is helpful to understand the
triggers we discussed earlier so that you are familiar with
your boss's hot and cold buttons. You can also speed the
process up if you have a little support in your endeavors.
If coworkers are also bothered by your Boss from Hell,
tell them about your behavior modification plan and get
them to do the same thing. It won't take long for your
boss to figure out which side her bread is buttered on.

Educate

A lot of the time, your Boss from Hell's unacceptable
behavior comes from a simple lack of awareness of the
impacts of her behavior. Often, she is so focused on herself and her own needs that she is completely oblivious
to the needs of those around her. Compounding the
problem is that people typically either don't know how,
or are afraid, to talk to her about it.

While it may not be a pleasant course of action, it is
sometimes possible to get your boss to reduce her negative

behavior simply by making her aware of the consequences of her actions, or at least by educating her so that she comprehends the magnitude of what it is she's asking for. Just make sure that you do it right. There are better and worse ways to say things, and, when it comes to talking with your Boss from Hell, make sure you present things in the best way possible. Avoid negative language, and try to frame your words with the tried-and-true "poop sandwich." The structure of the poop sandwich is good stuff–bad stuff–good stuff. Start with something positive, tell her what's really on your mind, then end with something positive. Beginning and ending with positives will help your boss to keep an open mind and reduce the chances of her becoming defensive.

To illustrate the difference your approach can make, let's take a look at the following examples. Assume, for a moment, that your boss happens to be the yelling and screaming type. You pick a time (when she's not yelling and screaming) to go into her office to tell her what the impacts of her actions are. Here are three different ways that you might approach it.

Bad: "I really wish you wouldn't yell and scream and carry on like you did yesterday." This is the direct approach. It is confrontational and will inevitably prompt a poor reaction from your boss.

Better: "Boss, I know you have really high standards, and you want everything to run smoothly around here. So do I. But, when you start yelling like you did yesterday, I get very flustered, and I can't do my job as well as I might. Do you think maybe you could not yell? That way I can do a better job." This approach uses the good-bad-good structure, but the choice of words could still have a negative effect.

Best: "I know that you have extremely high standards – the highest in the company, I expect – and I would really like to try to do my part to make sure that we can always meet those standards. One of the things I wanted to let you know about me is that, when you get very passionate like you did yesterday when nobody could find those file folders you were looking for, it has a very negative effect on me. I get flustered and feel defensive. I just thought you might want to know that the next time something like that comes up, because I really want to do my part to make sure that things are perfect, and I don't want to let you down." In this example, the positive sides of the poop sandwich have greater emphasis, and the language is gentler. "Yelling" is reframed as "being passionate," and the benefit to the boss of being a little less "passionate" is more clear. The situation is more clearly defined so that the boss will focus more clearly on the issue.

In using the sandwich technique like this, you are laying the motivation for her to change her behavior on your shoulders. You're not telling her that her behavior is bad; you're telling her that it's you who reacts badly to it. This way she'll be able to make some changes to her behavior without feeling attacked or as though she's giving in.

Sometimes your discussion with your Boss from Hell is purely for educational purposes. Your boss has asked you to take on a large task without giving you enough time to complete it or without seemingly recognizing the magnitude of what she's asking. In this case, you want to subtly let her know that you just don't have a magic wand that does the work for you.

Let's say that you work in a retail store and that a giant shipment of merchandise has just shown up. Your Boss from Hell casually looks over and asks you to have all the product unpacked and on the shelves by the end of your shift. The most common strategy is to start pointing out to your boss all the work that's involved in this seemingly easy task. You could say "But, boss, I can't do all that! I have to unpack it, check it against the way-bill, enter it into our point-of-sale system, find the shelves to put it on, move the inventory that's already on those shelves to a different place, price everything, put it on the shelves, and then take away all the packing material!" Those may well be the things you have to do, but if you simply highlight them like that it can come across to your boss as just complaining.

A better strategy is to try to educate your boss by asking relevant questions under the guise of unconditional willingness to do what she asks.

You:	Sure, boss, I'll do my best. Have you already checked the inventory against the packing slips?
Boss:	No.
You:	Have you entered it into our point-of-sale system?
Boss:	No.
You:	Has it been priced?
Boss:	No.
You:	It looks like there's about 400 pieces here – should they be priced individually or with a shelf talker?
Boss:	Individually priced.
You:	Where should I put the things that are on the shelves now?

As your boss answers the questions, she begins to become aware of the workload she is really putting on you. With any luck at all, she will either scale back her expectations of you or assign someone else to help you.

Part of the training I received from my secretary Franca was that you can't have two things with the same priority. I remember dropping something on her desk and telling her that I needed it by 4 p.m. She smiled sweetly at me and said "Maybe you can help me. The company president put this other thing on my desk, and he wants it for 4:00, and one of the VPs gave me another thing for 4:00. Would you mind talking with them to make sure it's OK to put yours ahead of theirs?" I often think that one of the reasons I didn't turn out to be a

Boss from Hell myself was largely because of Franca's training.

Set and Manage Expectations

One of the biggest mistakes I used to make in business was overpromising. I was constantly setting unrealistic deadlines and workloads for myself. For the most part, I always managed to deliver — but not without adding considerable stress and sleepless nights to my life. It was the administrative assistant of one of our clients who finally straightened me out.

She had asked me when she could expect a report on a project my company had completed for them. I cheerfully told her that we would have it to her by the end of the week. "Are you suicidal?" she said to me over the telephone. "Look, he's not expecting this report for two weeks. And even if he was expecting it earlier, his workload is so heavy he wouldn't be able to do anything with it for two weeks at the earliest. Don't kill yourself. Tell me you'll have it in two weeks. That way, if you have it to me by the end of the week, you'll look like a hero. And if something goes wrong in the next few days, you also have a bit of a buffer. The other thing," she said, "is that, if you deliver it in three days this time, he'll expect it in three days the next time. Take it from me if you want to keep from going crazy — learn how to manage the expectations that people will have of you." The lesson I learned was invaluable. Always try to give yourself a time buffer. If your boss has unrealistic or unfair expectations of you, the best way to change them is to retrain him as to what those expectations should be.

What can create challenges in these situations is when your boss has experience with somebody who was more proficient at something than you are. A secretary who typed faster than you. A salesperson who sold more than you. A programmer who programmed better than you. First of all, if that is in fact the case, understand that there's no shame in there being other people out there who are better than you at certain things. That's true for all of us. What's important is that your boss understands what his expectations of *you* should be. And as long as you live up to those expectations, you'll get less grief.

Make Molehills out of Mountains

Some bosses have a tendency to overreact — and it seems that everything your boss gets you involved with is at a crisis level. He works everyone into a frenzy, until everyone's nerves start to fray. It can often seem like quite odd behavior for someone in a managerial position. Why does he get like this? How does someone reach his level without being able to deal with difficult situations? Well, for starters, recognize that your boss isn't Superman. Like the rest of us, sometimes he needs a little reassurance and a sense of confidence from the people around him. Often he is overreacting because he's become too focused on all the negative possible outcomes. You can give him that confidence by consistently outlining situations in the most positive of lights and identifying all the options still open to you. Over time, you can eventually retrain him to focus more on the positives than the negatives.

Let's say you work for an automotive supply company, one of the parts you ordered for one of your customers hasn't arrived, and your boss is flipping out. You can reassure him by saying "Don't worry, boss, it's not that big of a deal. It's still early in the day, and I can call our supplier and have them ship it by same-day courier, and bingo — we have our part." You then continue to minimize his stress by outlining alternative plans B, C, and D. "Besides, boss, even if we don't get it today, we'll get it tomorrow, and our customer is only missing a day. It's not like it was our fault or anything! Worst-case scenario, we go to our competitor at the other side of town (I happen to know they have it in stock), buy the part from them, and then sell it to our customer. We won't make any money, but our customer will be happy." Your boss, now seeing that there are several possible solutions to the problem, becomes a little less panicky and a little more assured. After you've done this on two or three occasions, you begin to train your boss to believe that you do, in fact, have things under control and that he can trust you to do the right things.

The Straw Man Strategy

Finally, there is the straw man strategy, which is pretty much the opposite of the molehills out of mountains strategy. Reverse psychology, if you will. A straw man argument is a philosophical term to describe a creation that is easily knocked down. The principle, in this context, is to build on the premise created by your boss to such a point that even she herself begins to question her position. The straw man strategy, in the case of the missing automotive part, might go something like this:

> Oh, my goodness, you mean it's not here? That's horrible! We could lose this customer's business because of this! Who knows, if that part is for one of *their* best clients, they're really going to get ticked. The last thing we need is for them to start bad-mouthing us to all of our other customers! You know what, I ordered that part myself, and I have the proof. I'm not going to take the heat for something our supplier did! Oh, man, our customer is going to get really bent out of shape about this one, I can just feel it! And I'm the one who's going to be taking the heat for it. . . .

Your boss, on seeing *your* overreaction, will now begin working to comfort *you*. Often, when the molehills out of mountains strategy backfires on you, the straw man strategy will work like a charm.

If you go about it the right way, retraining your boss can actually become kind of a fun project. Plan it out — and even tell others what you are doing. Identify exactly the behaviors you are going to change in him, and set them as your goals. Track your progress. After a month or two goes by, see how much has changed. You might well surprise yourself at how much impact you can have on your boss's behavior.

CHAPTER NINE

STAND YOUR GROUND

As long as your position is based on a clear and
consistent set of ethics, you won't go wrong.

Many years ago, when I was in the advertising agency
business, a large client of ours in the banking industry
asked us to put together a promotional map so that their
customers could easily locate their automated banking
machines. My boss, the vice-president, told the client
that he would personally look after that since I was busy
looking after the production of a number of television
commercials for the client.

A couple of weeks later, in a planning session, I casually asked my boss how the ABM project was coming
along. "It's in the works," he assured me. I nodded,
although I hadn't seen any sign of "the works" anywhere
in the agency. I offered to take over the project for him,
but he assured me that it wasn't a problem and that he
would look after things. Another two weeks went by, and
again I asked him about the ABM project. Again he
assured me that things were "in the works." After six
weeks and several inquiries, I finally stopped asking.

Two months after the original request, we were sitting in a briefing session with the bank's senior management team. "What is the status of the ABM map?" the bank president asked my VP.

The VP became visibly flustered. Despite my frequent reminders, he had completely forgotten about the project. "Uh, that one has taken a little more time than we expected," he said, frantically grasping at straws. He mumbled some reference to "strategic considerations" and then turned to me for support: "Tell me, Shaun, where is that project?"

Now, I knew what he wanted me to say. He wanted me to confirm that, although delayed, the project was indeed "in the works." I was faced with an awkward decision. On the one hand, I could be a good team player and play along with my boss. On the other hand, I could stick with my "Honesty is the best policy" principle. I chose the latter.

"I'm not really sure," I said. I thought my VP was going to explode. I could see that he was seething inside.

"Do you not remember the project?" he said, giving me another opportunity to back him up.

I desperately wanted to respond with "You mean the one I've been reminding you about for the past six weeks?" Instead, I simply said "Yes, but I wasn't really involved with it."

The bank's marketing manager, who'd been reviewing

his notes, then spoke up, saying to my vp "Actually, you said you would be looking after this."

The shade of green my vp's face had turned was quite an interesting color.

When we got back to the agency, all hell broke loose. The vp stormed into my office and began a loud tirade about the importance of being a team player and how I'd left him hanging out to dry. Before I could reply, the agency's managing director ambled into my office and asked what the problem was. After hearing what had gone on, he turned to the vp and said very quietly "I think perhaps that we should have a conversation in my office." I never did find out what was said between the two of them, but I do know that for the rest of the day my vp's face had managed to find a shade of green even more interesting than the one before.

I suggested earlier that one of the important princi-ples of dealing with a Boss from Hell is to learn to pick your battles. As Kenny Rogers wrote in his song "The Gambler," "You've got to know when to hold 'em, and know when to fold 'em. Know when to walk away, and know when to run." In this case, I chose to stand my ground. But why this time? It wasn't the first time my Boss from Hell had done something stupid, but it was the first time I chose to stand my ground. The reason is that, in this instance, he was asking me to go against one of my fundamental personal principles — that, regardless of the consequences, lying is simply never an option.

And that is the rule for successfully standing your ground. As long as your position is based on a clear and consistent set of ethics, you won't go wrong. Consistency is essential. It is also critical that your position is founded on high-level principles and shared by those around you. Standing your ground will not work if you are inconsistent or if you base your decision on personal values that may not be shared.

I remember going to a party once. The host and hostess were warmly greeting people at the door, taking their jackets, and hanging them up. When one woman showed up wearing a mink coat, the hostess said coolly "You'll have to hang that one up yourself. I don't believe in killing animals to make fur coats." The owner of the coat became understandably embarrassed and offended, and everyone else at the party became uncomfortable. The hostess had chosen to stand her ground based on personal values and beliefs that weren't necessarily shared by the other people in the group. Even those who did share her point of view on furs thought that it was an inappropriate time, place, and manner of expressing it.

Stand your ground when you know that your position is completely defensible by you and others. People can easily accept, for example, an orthodox Jew politely refusing food made with pork when offered to him. It would be a different story, however, if the same orthodox

Jew went to a Pork 'r' Us restaurant and then complained about the food selection. People can respect a person who will not compromise family time for the sake of the job. But people will be less understanding if someone uses that rationale to refuse to work half an hour past 5 p.m. to bail out a coworker in serious trouble — especially if it's a coworker with a history of bailing out other people in need.

Presenting It Positively

When you do find yourself in a position where it's appropriate to stand your ground, it's important that it's done in the most positive way possible. Think of the example of my vp and me. When we were sitting around the boardroom with all of our client's eyes on us, I could easily have said "You're the one who took the project on, and I've been reminding you about it for six weeks!" The statement would have been true, but the wording would have been extremely embarrassing for him. You can turn down an offer to judge a beauty pageant by saying "No, thanks anyway, beauty pageants aren't for me." Or you can say "No, I won't judge this. I think that beauty pageants are sexist and exploitative." In both cases, you're standing your ground, but in the second case you're being confrontational.

If you're a vegetarian at a party, and someone offers you a plate of cocktail weenies, you could politely say "No, thanks, I'm a vegetarian," or you could say "No, I think it's wrong to eat the flesh of a living creature." Again the second option creates the risk of embarrassing or offending the host. Remember that old saying "It's not what you say; it's how you say it."

One good method of standing your ground is to present alternatives that your boss can live with. For example, if your boss is asking you to work late one night, but you have a personal commitment to always be home to cook supper for your kids, you might say "Gee, I can't work past five — I have to be home for my kids — but I can come in early tomorrow morning if that will help." The message your boss gets is that, while you won't compromise on the things that are important to you, you are still a team player.

Standing your ground, if nothing else, has a tremendous effect on your self-image. Even if it doesn't work, and your Boss from Hell continues to ignore your values and principles, there is great satisfaction in knowing that you haven't compromised the things that are important to you. Like the good guys in the movies, win or lose, you get to keep your honor.

TALK TURKEY

The ability to ask relevant, directed questions
is one of the most important communication
skills you can ever develop.

Occasionally you will run into a Boss from Hell with
whom, despite your best efforts, nothing works. You've
tried flying below her radar; you've tried ignoring her,
retraining her, and standing your ground, but your Boss
from Hell is still driving you nuts. It's time to talk turkey.

By the time you hit this stage, you have nothing to
lose. You're not enjoying your job, and the prospect of
things improving is bleak. The only thing left is to sit
down with your boss and tell her exactly how you're feeling. It's a worthwhile strategy to explore before you
resort to the end game of leaving the company (which
we'll discuss in the next chapter). Believe it or not, it is
frequently the case that a Boss from Hell truly does not
understand the impact that her actions are having on
those around her. And even if she is conscious that she's
pushing your buttons, she may not realize that she's
pushed you quite so far.

Here's how to do it. First, make sure that you pick the right time and place. The best time to talk turkey is at the beginning of the day, before your boss has the opportunity to get involved in the daily routine, and before something goes wrong that might put her in a bad mood. Go to work a little early. Be there, if you can, a little before the boss gets in. Try not to pick a day of the week that's just inherently going to be a bad day. For example, if you work in a retail store, don't pick a Saturday morning. If you work in an accounting department, don't do it at month end. Even the time of year can make a difference. If you work in a bank, you might want to avoid having the meeting at tax time. If you work for a florist, you'll want to avoid any time around Valentine's Day. Once you've decided on the time, choose a quiet place that offers minimal opportunity for disruptions. Finally, give your boss advance notice. In doing this, not only will she set the time aside, but she will also get the message that what you want to talk about is important.

Take Control

When you do go into the meeting, be well prepared. You want to ensure that your issues are addressed and that the discussion doesn't go sideways or get off topic. Maintaining control of a conversation or a meeting is simple enough if you've planned it and if you execute it properly. The secret is this: *the person asking the questions controls the conversation.*

It is a common misconception that the person who speaks the most eloquently or persuasively is the one who controls a conversation. Nothing could be further from the truth. It is, in fact, the person who speaks the *least* who dictates the direction and flow of a conversation. It all has to do with the questions you ask.

The best analogy I can think of is that of a lawyer in a courtroom. When a witness gets on the stand, it is, of course, the lawyer who is in complete control. And she achieves this control by asking the witness questions. The type of questions she asks dictates the testimony the witness gives. If a lawyer asks the wrong question, she gets the wrong answer, which can jeopardize her case.

Take, for example, a lawyer trying to prove that a witness has been cheating on his wife. She asks the question "Mr. Smith, have you had an affair with your secretary?" Mr. Smith honestly answers "No, I haven't." If, however, the lawyer asks the question "Mr. Smith, who have you had an affair with?" the only honest answer would be "With my next-door neighbor." Two similar questions with dramatically different results.

To demonstrate the power of questions in everyday life, try this exercise sometime. Out of the blue, ask someone what his favorite color is. Typically, he will pause for a moment to think before he answers you. During that brief pause, he is considering your question, which means that, in essence, you have just redirected his thought process. Chances are he wasn't thinking about colors before you asked him. But when you did, he paused and shifted his focus to the topic of your question. You literally controlled the direction of his thought. The ability to ask relevant, directed questions is one of the most important communication skills you can ever develop.

When you have your meeting with your Boss from Hell, the first thing you want to do is establish your value to her and the company. So your first question might be something like this: "You know what, boss, I've always had good performance reviews, but do you feel I'm pulling my weight around here?" Now, as any good lawyer will tell you, you should never ask a question that you don't already know the answer to. If you think that your boss's answer will be "No," then you probably shouldn't be going into her office in the first place. Reread Chapters 1 and 2 and review the things you have to do to meet your boss's expectations of you. If the answer is "Yes," then you have just successfully completed the first step. Your boss has now acknowledged your value to the company.

Your next step is to confirm your commitment to her and the company and have her acknowledge that commitment. You might say something like "You know, boss, I really want to do well for you, the team, and the company. . . ."

After the boss has confirmed to you that you're a wonderful person, identify her behavior and how it's impacting you, and then outline the message her behavior sends to you. For example, "When you say those really sarcastic things, I find it really demotivating, and the message I'm getting is that you don't particularly like me and that you don't particularly appreciate the things I'm doing."

Although this isn't worded in a traditional question format, it is, in fact, a question. It demands a response from your boss. She now has to do one of two things. Either she has to verbalize that she is, in fact, not happy with your performance levels, or she has to reaffirm your value to the company and to her. If she tells you that she's not satisfied with your performance, your next question becomes "What can I do to meet these expectations?" If she reaffirms your value to the company, your next question becomes "What can I do to avoid those sarcastic remarks?" Either way you have her coming up with solutions to the problem.

She may ask you about specific instances of her behavior, so be prepared. She may try to take control by asking a series of questions herself. Always be prepared to answer those questions with questions of your own. She might ask "Why do those sarcastic remarks bother you so much?" Instead of offering a convoluted answer, you could say "They just do — what's the purpose of them?" or "Does my behavior really warrant the sarcasm?"

At the end of your turkey-talking session, reaffirm your commitment to doing well, but mention that you really need things to improve for you to be happy. For example, "Like I said, boss, I really want to work hard and do well. But my motivation has really taken a hit — I hope that you understand." Your boss may or may not understand why you feel the way you do, but at least you've got it out in the open. It's up to her to make the decision whether or not you are important enough for her to change her behavior. If she doesn't change her behavior, then you really have only two options left: learn to live with your boss and the unhappiness she is creating, or seek alternative employment opportunities.

CHAPTER ELEVEN

EXIT STAGE LEFT

*He who fights and runs away will live
to fight another day.*

There's an old saying: "He who fights and runs away will live to fight another day." After you've tried everything, nothing has improved, and there's no relief on the horizon, the only real option open to you is to look for work elsewhere. While that decision can often be very stressful and scary, most people find they can look back on it as one of the best they've ever made. The thing about quitting, though, is that, if you're going to leave a company, you want to do it on your terms instead of your boss's. If you are unhappy with your work situation, and you stick around too long, your performance will begin to suffer. When your performance suffers, so do your annual reviews and any hopes for reasonable job references.

You want to join a new company when your performance is at its peak — not when it's at its lowest point. You also don't want to be in a position where your performance suffers so much that, instead of quitting, you get fired. To reiterate what I said at the beginning of the book, life is too short to spend 40+ hours a week in pain and misery. If you've tried everything and things still aren't getting any better — get out! You aren't doing yourself any favors by working for a boss you hate.

Far too often I see people who stick around in a job that is driving them nuts for far too long. If you ask them, they will tell you that they stay because of some sense of loyalty or because they like the other people around them. But the truth is there is usually only one reason people don't just quit their jobs and look for work elsewhere: fear. Fear of change. Fear of the unknown. What if I can't get a new job? What if I don't like the new job I get? What if I end up with a boss worse than the one I have now?

Yes, there is risk in changing jobs. Any time you make any change in your life there's risk. But the question you have to ask yourself is what's the risk if you *don't* make a change? What's the risk of continuing to work in an environment that you don't enjoy? One that's causing you stress. That's keeping you awake at night. That's impacting your personal relationships.

I think, once you take a close look at things, you'll discover that finding a new job is often the best option for both the short term and the long term. But before you just march into your boss's office and hand him your resignation, it is imperative that you are well prepared. There are a few proverbial ducks you want to have in a row — not the least of which is having a new job to go to.

Begin by contacting your network of people to see what, if anything, is available. If you work for a large company, this network might include your HR manager, who might know of some openings elsewhere in the company that you might enjoy. Meet with a few head-hunters, and spend some time updating your résumé. The process of finding a new job can sometimes take several months — so be patient.

It's also a good idea to ensure that there's someone at a senior level within your company whom you may be able to use as a reference. If not, contact people at previous companies whom you have worked with to ensure that they will give you good references. Suppliers with whom you have a positive relationship can also be a good source of both job leads and references.

Most importantly, take the time to decide what you really want to do. Conceivably, it's not your boss or your company you are disenchanted with — it's your occupation. A little introspection is a good way of avoiding a potentially unfortunate career move.

There are some good books out there on job searching, and I encourage you to read them to better prepare yourself for the journey. To get you started, though, here are some of the basics.

Your Résumé

1. *Tailor your résumé specifically for the company you are applying to.* Trying to use a one-size-fits-all résumé is a recipe for failure. Make sure that all the information is relevant to your prospective new employer.

2. *Ensure that your résumé highlights your strengths, not your weaknesses.* If you don't have a lot of work experience, but you have a strong educational background, lead with your education. If education is not your strong point, lead with your experience.

3. *Don't just list the companies you've worked for and how long you've worked for them.* Identify for each, with three lines maximum, any significant accomplishments or achievements you've had with that company. Don't be modest, but by the same token don't exaggerate or embellish.

4. *Give everything the "Who cares?" test.* If you're applying for a job in IT, don't put down that you enjoy playing soccer, football, and baseball. The person reading your résumé won't care.

5. *Don't put "Reason for leaving" on each job you've itemized on your résumé.* I remember getting a résumé once in which the applicant had written "Reason for leaving: my boss was a jerk." While it may well have been true, my first impression was that this was a person with attitude issues.

6. *Ask two or three of your friends to proofread and critique your résumé.* Proofreading is critical. Many prospective employers, me included, will throw a résumé into the recycling container the moment they see a typo. The message they get is that you don't

have great attention to detail.

7. *Don't put reference names on your résumé.* And don't put "References are available on request." Employers will assume that you have references and will ask for them later. However, if you do have one or two glowing *letters* of reference, feel free to staple them to the résumé.

8. *Try to keep your résumé to two neat, well-laid-out pages.* Your prospective employer just wants to get a glimpse of who you are — he's not looking for your autobiography.

Remember that the sole purpose of a résumé is to get you an interview — to get you through the door. It's a snapshot of you to help people determine if you're worth putting on the shortlist. Everything you put in it has to work toward achieving that goal.

Your Cover Letter

Your cover letter is your sales pitch. As such, it must be succinct, hard-hitting, and tailored specifically to the company you are approaching. Writing a standard, boiler-plated cover letter is a complete waste of your time. Have you ever had a telemarketer call you at home and begin reading a canned sales pitch? You know she's reading from a script, and you know it's the same script she's read a hundred times before to a hundred different people. You know that she knows nothing about you and that she doesn't really care about you. She just wants to make a sale. Think of how you feel when one of those people calls. It's the same way your prospective employer feels when he sees a boilerplate cover letter.

1. *Keep your cover letter to no more than two-thirds of a page.* Anything longer and there is the risk that your prospective employer may not read it. If your cover letter extends to two pages, it's almost guaranteed that he won't read it.

2. *Make sure it's been proofread.* And double-, triple-, quadruple-check the spelling of the contact's name and the company name.

3. *Make sure that it is organized properly.* Here are the 10 parts of the body of a good cover letter.

    i. Your first sentence should identify the purpose of your letter. There are many different ways to begin a cover letter, but I still haven't found one better than the tried-and-true "Please find attached a copy of my résumé for your consideration." It gets right to the point.

    ii. Your second sentence should be a statement of your greatest strength. Again, keep it simple and to the point; for example, "I am an electrical engineer with 12 years of senior management experience in the high-tech industry."

    iii. The third sentence should identify why you've chosen to send your résumé to that company in particular. "I am very interested in [company name] and its products."

    iv. The fourth sentence should be a statement about why the

company should be interested in you. "I believe that with my experience, and my understanding of the industry, I can be a tremendous asset to your company."

v. In your fifth sentence, make a statement about your work ethic and personality. "I'm a positive team player who is persistent and focused."

vi. In the sixth sentence, ask for the meeting. "I would greatly appreciate an opportunity to meet with you to discuss the potential of employment with [company name]."

vii. In your seventh sentence, reiterate your strengths and reassure your prospective employer that you won't be wasting her time. "I bring with me a tremendous amount of industry experience, and I'm confident that you will find the meeting productive."

viii. Then provide your contact information. "I can be contacted at [phone number]."

ix. Close the letter. "I look forward to hearing from you."

x. Sign off. "Sincerely, [your name]."

Here is how the sample letter looks in full.

Dear Ms. Smith:

Please find attached a copy of my résumé for your consideration.

I am an electrical engineer with 12 years of senior management experience in the high-tech industry. I am very interested in [company name] and its products. I believe that with my experience, and my understanding of the industry, I can be a tremendous asset to your company. I'm a positive team player who is persistent and focused.

I would greatly appreciate an opportunity to meet with you to discuss the potential of employment with [company name]. I bring with me a tremendous amount of industry experience, and I'm confident that you will find the meeting productive.

I can be contacted at [phone number]. I look forward to hearing from you.

Sincerely,

[your name]

4. *Make it look professional.* Have your cover letter printed on high-quality white paper. Resist the temptation to use colored paper, no matter how subtle you perceive the color to be. You might think that avocado green is just delightful, but your prospective employer may hate it.

5. *Send it by regular mail.* Buy a white 9"x12" envelope and mail your cover letter via regular post. Although e-mail is now a common way of communicating, and most prospective employers are used to getting résumés by e-mail, this is an instance in which low-tech beats high-tech.

6. *Build a tickler file.* A tickler file, or BF (Bring-Forward) File, is a method for ensuring that you follow up consistently and at the appropriate time. Follow-up is the key to success in finding a job. Most prospective employers receive a lot of résumés. Some of them get thousands every year. Your odds of getting an interview

are far less dependent on your qualifications than on how top of mind you are when a job opening does appear.

Although there are many electronic options for time and task management, this is another case in which I prefer a low-tech approach. Get a plastic index file and 12 cards headed with the 12 months. Now take 31 index cards and number them from 1 to 31 to represent the days of the month. Insert them behind the month you're currently in. When you mail a résumé, take another blank index card and write the name of the company across the top of it along with the contact name and her telephone number. Set your first follow-up date one week from mailing each résumé. So, for example, if you mail the résumé to ABC company on February 1st, place your index card behind your marker for February 7th. Make a habit of checking your tickler file each day to identify the people you need to contact.

Take out the index card, and make your call. If you're unable to reach the person, place the index card in the next day's slot. If you do reach the person, and there is currently no job available, ask her what might be an appropriate time to follow up. If she suggests that you should call back in a month, place the index card in the appropriate spot in the following month. Persistence is the key.

Show Time!

The minute you walk through the door for your interview, all of the wonderful things in your résumé become meaningless. At this point, you are now both the salesperson and the product, and your odds of getting work are directly related to how well you perform. Here are a few tips for maximizing your potential in your interview.

1. *Practice, practice, practice.* Don't assume that you're going to walk in there and knock them dead. Ask a friend if she wouldn't mind doing some role-playing with you in some mock interviews. Be prepared for the following questions.

   - *Why are you looking to change jobs?* Your answer has to be positive and upbeat. If you say something like "Because my boss is a jerk" or even "I don't quite see eye to eye with management," your interview is dead right there. Regardless of your skill or knowledge, most interviewers will shut you right down if they hear anything they perceive to be a negative attitude. Make sure your answer will be seen as a strength or benefit to the company. For example, "I'm looking to expand my understanding of the industry" or "I've heard wonderful things about this company, and from what I've heard I like the direction it's going." If you respond with something more neutral, such as "I'm just looking for a change of scenery," the interviewer will wonder, if you are hired, how soon you'll be looking for another change of scenery. Employers are looking for people who have the potential to be long-term, loyal employees. Don't be afraid to be positive!

   - *What do you know about our company?* Make sure that you've done your research and that you know what the company does.

- *What do you think you can do for this company?* This is a tricky one, and you have to answer it carefully. Whatever you do, don't outline what you perceive to be negative aspects of the company and how you're going to fix them. For example, don't say "Well, the company really needs to improve its customer service, and I think I can make a difference there." The interviewer may believe that the company already has excellent customer service, and she may consider you to be overly critical. It's also possible that customer service skills aren't what the company is looking for in a new employee. This is a great opportunity to take a little control of the interview by answering the question with a question. A good way to respond to this question is "I think I can bring a lot to the company in many different areas. Where do you see the greatest challenges at the moment?"

- *What are your long-term goals?* Again you have to be careful. You don't know if the company is looking for someone who is ambitious or someone who is just looking to work hard. When this question is asked, it's a great opportunity to convey your positive attitude and your eagerness to do well. For example, you could say "You know what – I'm not exactly sure what my long-term plans are. I just really love doing what I do, and I'm anxious to learn as much as I can at this stage."

2. *The more questions you ask, the better.* Preplan your questions. Make sure they relate to what you can do for the company, not what it can do for you. Asking questions such as "What would my salary be?" or "What's the benefit package?" or "How much vacation time

will I get?" or "How much freedom will I have?" are red flags to prospective employers. They are signals that you are focused on yourself, not on the company. Remember that, at this stage, you're trying to sell the company on you. Not until you've accomplished that do you want to hear its sales pitch to you. Here are some questions you can ask.

- What are you looking for the person in this position to be contributing to the company?
- Is there anything new and exciting in the works with the company?
- How big is the team I'd be working with?
- And here's the best one. "What are you looking for in an employee in this position?" If the interviewer gives you the answer, all you have to do is be that person, and you've got the job.

Asking questions helps you to take control of the interview and ensures that it moves in a direction that works in your favor.

Deciding to leave your place of employment is a big step. It's stressful and can sometimes be a little scary. As long as you're doing it for the right reasons, however, it's worth the risk. I can't count the number of people who have said to me "I wish I'd changed jobs years ago!"

PART THREE

Hell on Wheels

Because this beast, at which thou criest out,
Suffers not any one to pass her way. But so
doth harass him, that she destroys him; And
has a nature so malign and ruthless, That never
doth she glut her greedy will, And after food is
hungrier than before.

— Dante's *Inferno*

CHAPTER TWELVE

STUPID BOSS TRICKS – AND HOW TO BEAT THEM

No one has ever fired someone for being too happy,
too enthusiastic, or too motivated. Remember that.
If he gets on your nerves, kill him with kindness.

In the first two parts of the book, we focused on the
things you can do to ensure that you're a better
employee and on some general strategies for dealing
with some general Boss from Hell types. Let's face it,
though, Bosses from Hell can come in so darned many
shapes and sizes that sometimes general strategies simply don't work. In this section, we're going to take a look
at 19 specific types of Bosses from Hell and some strategies for dealing with them. They are divided into three
categories: scary, stressful, and annoying.

Scary Bosses from Hell

Scary Bosses from Hell are those one-in-a-thousand
bosses who actually give the impression that they enjoy
being as miserable as they are. They subscribe to the MBA
(management by abuse) theory of management, and

they are generally people who never should have been given power in the first place. In this section, I outline six of them.

1. The Exploder

Like all Bosses from Hell, the Exploder has certain triggers that set him off. Unlike other Bosses from Hell, however, when this one goes off, the explosion can be heard throughout the workplace. There is no gradual buildup and often no warning. His rant is sometimes so incoherent that you have to make a concerted effort just to understand what the issue is. The Exploder doesn't need a particular person at whom to direct his explosion. He can explode when he's all by himself. But even if his tirade isn't directed toward you, you and everyone else within earshot become uncomfortable. It's not unusual for the Exploder to be an otherwise quiet person, so the contrasting outbursts seem even more dramatic.

There are two common reasons for explosive behavior: (1) the Exploder doesn't deal with issues on an ongoing basis, so they accumulate in his psyche, creating a situation in which the slightest thing can set him off; (2) exploding is a defensive strategy that sends the clear message to people "Stay away from me, and don't do anything to tick me off."

Simply talking with the Exploder, and explaining to him how his behavior affects you, will rarely work. He sees his occasional aberrant behavior as just part of his personality — part of who he is. And while he may recognize that by normal social standards his behavior is wrong, he feels either that he is incapable of change or that change is unnecessary.

The best strategy I've heard of for dealing with an Exploder is to try, as much as possible, to make him at least a little self-conscious of his behavior. He'll still explode, but over time his explosions may become shorter and less frequent. One effective way of making him feel self-conscious is to convey to him that his behavior is causing him to lose the respect of the people around him.

One secretary I know once brought a tape recorder into work without her boss knowing and recorded him in a particularly juicy tirade. Early the next morning, before the boss came in to work, she put the cassette tape on the center of his desk on top of a piece of paper on which she had typed "Listen to me." According to the secretary, the boss never did identify who had recorded it, but his tirades were toned down after that. Her anonymous tape trick accomplished two things. First, it gave her boss an opportunity to hear himself and how silly he really sounded. Second, it sent a loud and clear message that everyone around him considered his behavior inappropriate.

Another thing you can try is to start making jokes

about the Exploder around the workplace. "Hey, have you heard about the new Harvey doll? You play with it for 10 minutes, and then it explodes." Or "How about that new Harvey doll — fun to play with, but it keeps losing its head?" Or "How many Harveys does it take to screw in a lightbulb? Two. One to screw in the bulb, and another one to scream randomly at nothing in particular." Once you've accumulated a bunch of little jokes like this, type them up and leave them on his desk one day. If Harvey begins to believe he's becoming the brunt of all the office jokes, he may try to change his behavior.

2. The Extortionist

The Extortionist is a classic example of someone who knows the power she wields and isn't afraid to abuse it. She works on the leverage that her position power gives her. She knows she controls your salary, your opportunities for advancement, your bonuses, your vacation time, your work environment, and, to a great extent, your happiness. And she will use all those levers for her own gain. If, for example, you decline her request to work late, she'll respond with "How badly do you want that promotion anyway?" or "Have you forgotten that your annual evaluation is coming up?" If you balk at her asking you to do something that you consider to be unethical, she'll remind you of how easily you can be replaced. She often couches her threats in a lighthearted manner so that, if you ever take her to task on them, she can come back with a roll of the eyes and a petulant "I was just joking."

The Extortionist is a particularly nasty type of Boss from Hell because she makes you feel so helpless. Even leaving the company is an unpleasant option for you because she's the one whom prospective new employers will be phoning for a reference. The Extortionist is into power and is very aware of who wields the power around her. The most effective way I know of to deal with the Extortionist is to make her aware of the power *you* wield.

You do this by following her lead and using her own techniques against her. She might say, for example, "Of course you can work an extra two hours, John. After all, I still haven't decided whether or not to give you those two weeks in July you asked for." You can respond, with a big smile on your face, "Oh, I know. But I still haven't decided yet if I'm going to bail you out on this rush job for our customer!" You've now sent her the message "I have a little power of my own," and it won't go unnoticed.

Once you've sent the message, drop it. You don't want to turn the situation into a standoff because, if it's a tie, you'll lose. If she challenges you on it, simply say "I was just joking." Whether she acknowledges it publicly or not, your message will still register with her. After you've done this a few times, you'll find that she won't use her extortionist techniques on you as often.

3. Nasty and Vindictive

A VP at one of the advertising agencies I once worked in had a true mean streak. A recently hired art director had unwittingly parked in a spot we all knew to be the VP's. When the VP walked through the front doors of the office, the first words out of his mouth were "Some moron has parked in my spot!"

The receptionist looked out and recognized whose car it was and said, "Would you like me to go get him and have him move it?"

"No, that's OK," the VP said, "I'm going to park behind him. He's not going to be able to get out until I do, and I'm going to be in meetings until 7:00 tonight. By the way," he added, "if he wants me to move my car, tell him I can't be disturbed."

The poor art director ended up waiting until 8:30 to get his car out. When he approached the VP at the end of his meeting, the VP responded with pure innocence. "Oh!" he exclaimed. "Was that *your* car?"

A retail sales rep I know once publicly disagreed with a regional sales manager and promptly found his shifts cut back to almost nothing. Another person I know once actually called in the police to file a missing person report when an employee was two hours late for work. The Nasty and Vindictive boss is basically a schoolyard bully moved into the working world. He throws his weight around, comforted in the knowledge that most people are too afraid to fight back.

As in the schoolyard, the best way to deal with these people is with a show of your own strength. You don't want to directly confront or threaten them, but you do want to send a subtle but clear message that you're not someone to be messed with.

In casual conversation, tell a story about how you yourself did something nasty and vindictive. It doesn't matter whether the story is true or not; what matters is that the message gets to your boss. The art director I mentioned above demonstrated clearly how this works. He came into work 15 minutes late one day, a month after the parking spot incident. The vp asked him where he'd been, and the art director told him that he'd had to take his car into the shop to have the rear end fixed. When the vp asked him what had happened, he explained that someone on the highway had been tailgating him — so, to teach him a lesson, he'd just hit the brakes, and the other car had slammed into his.

After the meeting, I said to the art director, "Wow, that's something I've always dreamed of doing but never had the courage to do!"

He grinned and said, "Neither did I. My car's really just getting a tune-up, that's all. I just want that @#$% vp to think I'm a little crazy so he won't mess with me again!"

Sure enough, the vp backed right off and never bothered him again.

4. Ethically and Morally Challenged

Every now and then you encounter a boss who's just plain slimy. You've seen him lie a hundred times to customers, coworkers, and employees. He'll fudge numbers and cheat at every chance he gets. The credo of Ethically and Morally Challenged Bosses from Hell is "It's only wrong if you get caught."

Working for these bosses creates several challenges. First, you may find yourself an accomplice to the things he does, thus compromising your own values. Second, even if you don't become an accomplice, there is the real danger of guilt by association, with people just assuming you are as ethically and morally challenged as he is. Third, you have that uncomfortable feeling of having to watch your back all the time.

My personal belief is that, if you end up working for such a boss, there is really only one viable option — and that is to get away as fast as you can. It's unlikely you'll change him, and no amount of reframing on your part will make his behavior easier to bear. The cost of working for an ethically and morally challenged boss is enormous. It affects your pride, your self-image, and your relationships with everyone around you. It's hard to imagine anything being worth that high a price.

If you do choose to stay with him, then covering your butt becomes an absolute necessity. Create a paper trail for everything, and always ensure that he's the one making all the decisions. Be unwavering with your principles without being confrontational. Make it clear that, as far as his unethical behavior is concerned, he's on his own. When potentially compromising situations occur, simple statements such as "I'm not going to lie" or "I'm not going to break the law" make it clear where you stand without giving him the impression of a condemnation or threat. Don't bother scolding him or correcting his behavior — it will serve no point. But do make sure that your own behavior is absolutely above reproach.

5. The Blamestormer

The Blamestormer's credo is "It doesn't matter if you win or lose; it's where you place the blame." Whenever anything goes wrong, her first priority is to look for a handy scapegoat. Actually correcting the problem is the last thing on her mind. Needless to say, the blame never seems to fall on her. It's as though she spends her entire life walking around with all of her fingers pointed outward.

Blamestormers have a heightened sense of self-preservation and will do virtually anything to avoid taking blame. If the information in the chapter "Covering Your Butt 101" doesn't help, try the following approach.

The next time you get blamed for something that isn't really your fault, try the "accept and react" technique. This tactic has two parts. The first stage is to simply accept the blame the boss has placed on you, without getting defensive or confrontational. The second is to ask her to identify specifically what you should do the next time a similar situation occurs so that you don't make the same "mistake" twice. In trying to respond to you, she will be forced to acknowledge things that may have been out of your control.

For example, imagine you're a receptionist, and your boss gives you a very important document to have couriered out for delivery the next morning. You call the delivery company, and the driver picks up the package, but it doesn't get delivered the next day as promised.

Your blamestorming boss may say "What the heck did you use ShipFast for? Everyone knows that they're useless! Did I not tell you that this was an important document? Now our client doesn't have it — and you have totally screwed things up!"

Rather than become defensive and point out that ShipFast is the courier your company has an account with, or the more obvious point that things are pretty much out of your control after a package has left your hands, begin by simply taking the blame. "Yes, boss, you're right. I know how important that package was."

A little later, though, when she has settled down, find a public spot to say to her, "Look, boss, I'm really sorry about that ShipFast delivery. Which company should I use in the future?"

When she answers, ask her, "Do we have a corporate

account with that company?"

She'll have to acknowledge that you don't.

Then you say, as nicely and sweetly as you know how, "I'm not sure, once the package has left our office, how to track it to make sure that it isn't in the process of getting lost. You indicated that there should be a way I can do that. Can you tell me how?"

Your boss will have no choice but to acknowledge, publicly, that it was unrealistic to expect you to control every stage of the shipment.

One thing to recognize about the typical blame-storming boss is that, while she enjoys assigning blame to others, she doesn't respond well when blame appears to be shifting to her. Becoming defensive, therefore, is your worst possible strategy. If you do, she'll simply use that against you by saying something like "You always have an excuse, don't you?"

6. The Credit Stealer

Many bosses out there like to take credit for the accomplishments of their employees. And sometimes they are absolutely blatant about it. Whether it is an idea you had, or one of your personal success stories, by the time your boss gets around to telling someone else about it, he's the hero. It's frustrating when you see him advance in an organization on the strength of your work. It becomes a serious issue when it starts to affect your opportunities for reward or advancement.

The best way I know of to deal with the Credit Stealer is to be direct. Let him know that you know what he's doing. You don't have to get nasty; you simply have to point out that you are aware of what he's done and that you aren't particularly happy. Find a private place, where it is just the two of you, and bring the subject up.

Imagine, for example, that you're an account manager, and you've come up with an idea to realign the account management group to make it more streamlined. You tell your boss about it, then discover later that, when he presented it to senior management, they were thrilled with the idea, but your name was never mentioned.

Here's how you might address it with your boss: "Hey, boss, I understand that the senior executives liked *your* idea to realign the account management group. It sounded very familiar. I was just wondering if, at some point, you were going to mention that I was in any way involved in this."

Your boss, caught in the act, will now have to dance a bit. Most likely he'll try to sell you on an explanation such as "Well, when I said 'I,' I really meant 'we,' and the senior executive really understood that." And he'll undoubtedly tell you that it's his full intention to let the senior managers know about your contribution.

Whether or not he's telling the truth is unimportant at this stage. He knows that he's been caught and will be less likely to try to steal credit from you again. Most Credit Stealers get away with their actions because nobody speaks up. Having said this, it's important to emphasize that you don't want to press the issue too much. If you do, looking for some short-term benefit, you may find yourself paying for your actions in the long term. He is still your boss, after all.

Stressful Bosses from Hell

Stressful Bosses from Hell are those who seem to be intent on creating ulcers in the people around them. In this section, I outline five of them.

1. Pile-On

Some bosses just don't seem to be happy unless they see huge piles of paper on your desk or impossible work-loads. It doesn't matter how much work you have; they'll give you more. They may recognize that you're over-worked or overburdened, but they'll give no indication that they care in the least.

One of the common symptoms of having a Pile-On boss is the creeping increase in the number of hours you work each week. It begins with you working through lunches and breaks. Then you start coming in half an hour early each morning and leaving late to try to get your work done. But just when you feel as though you're getting ahead of the game — whump! — there he is with another project for you.

The best way to deal with a Pile-On boss is to force him to prioritize your work for you. Keep on your desk at all times a piece of paper with a list of all the projects you currently have on the go. Beside each project, write down the amount of time you estimate it will take to accomplish it. The next time your boss walks by and plops yet another project down on your desk, nicely ask him for a couple of minutes of his time to help you sort something out. Show him your list and the time frames involved, and have him help you to prioritize the tasks. In that simple process of just doing the math, three things will happen. First, your boss will recognize that he has to either reduce your workload or increase the amount of time he gives you to get things done. Second, he will better appreciate the amount of work you are doing for him. And third, he'll think twice the next time he plans to throw a new project at you.

2. The Slave Driver

Like the Pile-On Boss from Hell, the Slave Driver expects you to be at his beck and call at virtually all times. He won't hesitate to ask you to work nights, weekends, and holidays, and he'll express great disappointment any time you object. The Slave Driver isn't shy about what he does to his people. In fact, he'll often wear it like a badge of honor. And, where the Pile-On Boss from Hell is simply trying to squeeze every last drop of productivity out of you, the Slave Driver enjoys exercising his power.

The Slave Driver is often a bit of a workaholic himself. His sole focus is on getting things done, regardless of the costs to the people who work for him. He doesn't mind taking on a heavier workload because ultimately he's not the one doing all the work. What makes the Slave Driver difficult to deal with is that he usually has several people working for him — all working the same stupid hours he's asking you to work. When you try to point out to him that you'd like your life to include things other than work — little things such as sleeping, eating, breathing — he'll point to your coworkers and give you an "Are you part of the team, or aren't you?" speech.

Jill, a secretary in a high-tech firm, recounted to me a classic example of a Slave Driver in action. It was the Friday before a long weekend, and she had told her boss that, if at all possible, she would like to leave half an hour early to avoid the rush on the way up to her cottage. There was going to be a surprise 40th birthday party for a good friend, and she wanted to give herself plenty of time to make it. Her boss had just smiled at her and said "We'll see what we can do."

As it turned out, Jill didn't get out of the office until 6:30. According to her, the work her boss had her doing was trivial and in no way urgent, but he'd insisted that it get done before she left. "I should have known better," she said to me. "I've watched him do that to dozens of other people before."

For the Slave Driver, it is very important that everything you do is on his terms. Any hint that you would like to do your job on your terms will be met with instant resistance. The best way to deal with a Slave Driver is to adopt an indirect, passive-aggressive approach. Play his game for a little while, but when his requests become extreme simply don't play along.

In Jill's case, for example, her best strategy would have been to work right up until 5:00, then pack up and leave. Because she didn't leave half an hour early like she wanted, the Slave Driver, although not happy, would have nothing concrete to give her a hard time about. If, on the Tuesday, he chastises her for not having the work completed on the Friday, her response could be an innocent look, along with "Oh, I'm sorry! I just assumed that, since I wasn't able to get away half an hour early like I asked, it would at least be OK for me to leave at 5:00." The Slave Driver boss won't be happy about it, but the message has been sent. In a nonconfrontational manner, Jill has communicated that she can be pushed only so far.

This tactic is effective, although it's important that you don't use it too often. If you do, then the Slave Driver may begin to perceive a threat to his power. If that happens, he may feel the need to push things to even more uncomfortable levels.

3. Roadblock

While conducting a training program for a large national retailer, I encountered a particularly exceptional store manager. She was articulate, intelligent, and enthusiastic. Her team was positive and energized, and her store consistently exceeded its targets. She'd been with the company for three years.

In conversation with her boss, the district sales manager, a few weeks later, I suggested that this manager might be worth considering as a district sales manager herself. The DSM said to me "I know — she's amazing! But I don't put her name forward because I don't have anyone to replace her." This DSM had even gone so far as to hide job postings from the manager to prevent her from applying. The DSM was a Roadblock. She had someone working for her who made her look good, and she didn't want to lose her.

Roadblocks are typically very self-focused and insecure people with little or no regard for the impacts of their actions on their employees. Some are like the DSM, just trying to protect valuable resources. Others feel threatened by high-performing employees and want to "keep them in their places." Regardless of the motivation behind such actions, there is really only one effective way to deal with a Roadblock, and that is to be direct with her about your goals and aspirations.

Let her know, as nicely as you can, that you intend to achieve your goals with or without her. Instead of being confrontational, however, you accomplish this by enlisting her support. You can say, for example, "Boss, I've been doing this job for three years now, and I think I'm ready to move on to bigger things. I've set my goal to have a DSM job by the end of the year, either with this company or some other company — obviously I would prefer it's with this company. Can you tell me which things I might need to work on in order to achieve that?"

In using this approach, you communicate to your boss that your patience is wearing thin at not being promoted; that, if the company doesn't do anything, it's going to lose an employee; and that you respect and want her input.

As your "deadline" approaches, and still nothing has happened, reapproach your boss: "Boss, I don't know if you remember, but six months ago I told you that I was hoping to be in a position for a promotion by now. I was just wondering, what is the likelihood of an opportunity coming up in the near future with this company?" Again, instead of confronting your boss and demanding a promotion, you are simply asking her for advice. The message also carries a subtle "or else" submessage. Your boss will recognize that she now has to make a decision.

4. The Games Master

The Games Master is a Boss from Hell who seems to get his kicks by playing games with his employees — manipulating them and playing with them as though they were pawns in some bizarre chess game. He hints at phantom promotions and other "opportunities" to see how fast he can get them to move. He excludes key people from important meetings just to see how they will react. His little ploys are often used to achieve a variety of hidden agendas, but there are a lot of times too that the Games Master will play with people for no other reason than he can.

My first job out of university was selling advertising space for a local newspaper. On my first day, the publisher sent me out to approach a local car dealership. "This one's a sure thing," he said. "All you have to do is bring back the order."

Dutifully, I sped off to the dealership, excited about making my first sale. When I got to the dealership, I shook hands with the manager and said, "I understand you're interested in putting an ad in our paper."

A little grin spread on his face, and he said to me, "Am I now?"

I knew I was in trouble.

As it turned out, the dealership had never advertised in the paper, and the manager had no intention of doing so now. My publisher, however, made it a practice of sending every new hire off to see him, making the new guy feel as foolish as I did. As far as I could tell, there was no discernible reason for him to do this to us. But after watching him do it to a few people hired after me, I discovered that he always had a good laugh as the rookies went dashing out of the office to make their "first sale."

I know of one boss who, a month or so before annual review time, would give his employees an impossible task so that they would fail miserably at it. When review time came, he used this failure as leverage to deny them raises. One sales manager I know used to hold back credit approvals for new customers so that the salespeople wouldn't meet their monthly targets.

The Games Master is one of those bosses you can never quite bring yourself to trust — because you've watched him do too many things to too many people. What makes the Games Master so stressful is that it is very hard to catch him in the act or to *prove* that he's done anything *intentionally* wrong.

The best way I know to deal with the Games Master is to let him know you're on to him — without, of course, being confrontational or accusatory. If you sense he is playing some kind of game with you, do whatever you can to block it. In the instance of the sales manager who is holding back credit approval to prevent having to pay out bonuses, you might say "Jeepers, John, I would have thought that by now you would have come up with a more creative way of keeping us from getting our bonuses." Although your boss will deny it vehemently, he'll get the message that you're on to him, and he'll be less likely to continue with the practice.

5. The Invisible Man

Your boss uses all of the popular buzzwords. He "empowers his employees" and "entrepreneurializes" them. He lets them make decisions and work on sensitive projects. The only problem is that, when things show the slightest signs of going awry, he will distance himself from them faster than a nudist from a cloud of mosquitoes.

I once watched a senior marketing director for a shopping center developer give everything she had on a high-profile project. It was a project that everyone in the company at one time had been clamoring to be associated with. When word came down that the project might be scrapped, however, her bosses led the stampede away from it, leaving her holding the proverbial bag. Another example is a retail manager I know who magically evaporates every time a Customer from Hell comes into the store, leaving the employees to deal with him themselves.

The Invisible Man is an opportunist. He is adept at jumping on and off bandwagons, and he won't hesitate to hide behind the most convenient person, usually an employee, to avoid being associated with any sort of failure. Despite what he professes, his actions convey that he is loyal only to himself. He will deny having told you things or given you instructions. He will be nowhere in sight when you face a challenge.

This type of Boss from Hell can create tremendous stress in our lives because he makes us so vulnerable. It's a very disconcerting sensation when you know that there is no one watching your back. Unfortunately, you can fall into a common trap when coping with the Invisible Man as a boss. Because he's never there to protect you when you stick your neck out, it can be very tempting to stop sticking your neck out altogether. You reduce your activity to a minimum, and your performance never rises above mediocrity.

The Invisible Man has a strong preference for avoiding conflict. And, consequently, the best strategy for dealing with him is to make it more painful for him to avoid the conflict than to face it. This approach often means finding ways to drag him — sometimes kicking and screaming — into the situation. For example, when that Customer from Hell drops by and your boss has magically evaporated, give the customer your boss's name and tell her that he'd like to deal with the problem personally. Have the customer wait the extra 10 minutes or so until your boss reappears. The effect of this is that, not only does your boss have to deal with the upset customer, but the customer will now be even more upset after having been made to wait. Your boss may not be happy, but at least he will have to deal with the situation.

In a situation where your boss denies knowing anything about a project or having given you any instructions, stand your ground. You will find that as soon as you start publicly protesting — "Sure, don't you remember us talking about that? You said . . ." — he will usually back down and quickly try to change the subject.

Annoying Bosses from Hell

Not all Bosses from Hell are dangerous or creators of stress. Some of them just get on our nerves — constantly. Annoying Bosses from Hell are the ones with those certain idiosyncrasies and twitches that drive us nuts. They usually aren't intentionally trying to irritate people — it's just the way they are. Following are eight of my favorites.

1. Condescending

The Condescending Boss from Hell has that uncanny knack of being able to make the most innocent of comments express the sentiment that you're a moron. He can even make a compliment sound like a condemnation. He's the comic-book store owner on TV's *The Simpsons*. A simple "Nice job" from him can send the clear message that he believes anyone else in the world could have done the job better than you. Yet, if you take him to task, he will reply with something like "All I said was 'nice job.' I don't understand how you can find that offensive." He is smug, smarmy, and self-important. His arrogance really begins to get under your skin when it's clear that there is nothing to support it — that he really has nothing to feel superior about.

The temptation with the Condescending boss is to try to "prove" to him that you're not as stupid as he thinks you are. You become defensive and sometimes overcompensate — but to no avail. The fact is it doesn't matter how hard you try; this particular Boss from Hell will always look at the things you do with a certain amount of disdain.

You see, despite the seemingly aggressive stance, his actions are really more of a defense mechanism than anything else. As long as he can convince himself that he's above everyone else, he feels no threat from anyone. He gets a certain calmness and satisfaction from believing that he is superior in some way to most people. "Oh, sure," he'll tell himself, "there are people who have had greater successes than me, but I am still much smarter than they are. Of course, if I wanted to, I could have their successes too." Even when you, his employee, do have a success, he'll believe he could have achieved it himself as well. Although he'll never verbalize it, he perceives everything as a competition. And in the little world he has created, he will always win.

The only way I know to combat the Condescending Boss from Hell is with a little well-placed, self-effacing sarcasm. For example, when your boss says "Nice job" with that special tone of voice, look him in the eye, smile broadly, and say something like "Yeah, even we stupid people can do something right every now and then!" This response lets him know that you are aware of how he thinks, and that you think his attitude trivial enough to make a joke about it. The message he gets, in a non-confrontational way, is that you don't see the world — and him — the same way he does. In a sense, you are giving him the very feedback he is trying to avoid: judgment.

While this tactic may not always be effective in stopping his behavior — he has, after all, been doing it for a long time — it will at least remove the annoyance factor. His words will have far less impact on you when you're able to make light of the source.

2. Wet Fish

My company had been asked to conduct a needs analysis of the performance in one of our client's branch offices. Internal surveys had indicated that morale was low and that motivation was an issue. My first hint of where the challenges lay occurred when I shook hands with the branch manager. "Limp" wouldn't do his handshake justice. As I grasped his cool, lifeless, boneless fingers, I had the distinct sensation of holding uncooked frog's legs. His bland, expressionless face conveyed even less emotion than his colorless eyes. In our subsequent conversations, I discovered him to be both extremely intelligent and knowledgable. But, even when talking about things he felt strongly about, there was an absolute absence of passion.

In talking with his employees, I discovered that this mind-numbing demeanor was his trademark and remained virtually unchanged regardless of the circumstances. No one could remember him ever disciplining an employee; no one could remember him ever praising an employee. There was no recognition of initiative and at times no apparent recognition that the employees even worked for him. When head office had recently introduced an exciting new product line, it had launched it to all the company managers with a glitzy, high-energy ceremony. The employees in this office found out about it through a two-sentence memo.

All Staff:

Please be advised that XYZ Company is introducing a new line under the brand ClearSoap. Please be prepared to field customer inquiries.

The Wet Fish can suck energy and enthusiasm out of an environment faster than a mortician at a party, and the ensuing workplace tedium can make the days seem endless. This type of Boss from Hell has spent a lifetime flying below the radar. He is happy with what he has, and he believes that everyone else should be happy with what they have as well. He likes the status quo and avoids making decisions at all costs. He's learned that, if you avoid things long enough, they usually go away.

I know the general manager of a large retail company who is a master of doing nothing. He will go to extraordinary lengths to avoid making decisions or to take actions with the remotest risk attached to them. Instead of firing employees, he transfers them to different parts of the company. Rather than take corrective action when stores don't achieve their mystery shopping evaluation targets, he simply lowers the standards so that more stores are in compliance. Any new company initiatives — inevitably spearheaded by his boss, the company president — are assumed by the GM only with great reluctance. The semiannual regional manager meetings, which used to be fun and motivational, are now dry and uninteresting. Employees who are ambitious, creative, or energetic are driven to distraction.

The one thing I have learned about the Wet Fish is that it's unlikely anything you do will make him change. He is a professional risk avoider, a politician of sorts, and his behavior is reflected in every aspect of his life. You can, however, do things in spite of him. Remember that, as long as you pose no direct or indirect threat to him, you can pretty much get away with anything. If you're looking for a little more fun at work, organize an informal company event. If you think something needs to get done, just do it — as long as you're the one taking the risk, he won't care. Don't be afraid to stand out or even be a little outrageous — just leave him out of it.

3. Consensus Seeker

The Consensus Seeker is like a Wet Fish with a personality. She is often charming, intelligent, and positive in her management style. She will drive you crazy, however, when it comes time to make a decision.

The Consensus Seeker has confused a progressive, consultative management style with believing that she needs to have consensus on every decision. She will consult with her people on even the simplest of decisions and not reach a conclusion until absolutely everyone is in agreement. Although she is never controversial, she is also anything but effective.

The Consensus Seeker thinks that she's doing the right thing. She sees the never-ending consultation process as a way to keep people involved and give them ownership in the company's direction. She tries to ensure that she's viewed an issue from many different perspectives in order to arrive at the proper conclusions. Her Achilles heel is that she is also looking for the same committees to make her decisions for her. And we all know that, if there is one thing that committees are notoriously bad at, it's making decisions.

When she finally does make a decision, she typically won't stick with it for long. She's big on "flavor-of-the-month" actions — doing things that make her appear progressive and forward thinking. What makes the Consensus Seeker so annoying is the inertia she creates. She will ask you to come up with a myriad of plans and ideas but will waffle when it comes time to put them in action. When she does put your plan in action, she rarely gives it enough time to have the effect it should.

Remember that she's convinced her methods represent a proper, progressive management style designed to create a happier, more productive workplace. The best way to deal with her, therefore, is to present her with a logical argument that suggests you are neither happy nor productive. Using a variation of the poop sandwich, let her know that you are frustrated with her committee approach to all of her decisions. Give her memorable examples of several instances, but make it clear that you respect her efforts toward positive management. Here's how you might present it:

Hey, boss, I have a thought I wanted to share with you. You know how you make such an effort to get feedback from everyone before we implement things? I think there might be one or two things in which you should just let your own experience be your guide. Usually, the group comes to the same decision that you would anyway — like in instances X, Y, and Z. But, if you remember, it took us forever to actually get anything done. The thing is that I, for one, respect your judgment and any decisions you might make. I think the others do too.

In using this approach, you both communicate your interest in speeding things up and let her know that you respect her judgment and will abide by her decisions. The next time an issue comes up, and it looks like she is again going to seek group consensus, say something like "I'll go along with whatever you decide." Doing so will confirm what you suggested earlier and make it more comfortable for her to make a decision without the group.

4. The Pig

Sometimes it's basic personal hygiene. Sometimes it's a filthy office. Sometimes it's personal mannerisms that are just plain unacceptable. I have heard stories about bosses so disgusting that I can't even bring myself to write about them.

The boss of a friend of mine left for a three-week vacation. By the end of the first week, the smell from his office had grown so bad that employees broke the lock to get inside. In his desk drawer, they found over a week's worth of half-eaten egg salad and tuna sand-wiches. Another boss I know wouldn't change his shirt for a week at a time. We used to watch with fascination as the stain he acquired on a Monday would grow in size and shape throughout the week. By the Friday, no one would approach him because of his odor. One of my company's clients tells of a former boss who, no matter the social situation, couldn't speak without inserting a profanity into every sentence.

Pigs are bosses who simply don't seem to care about how others perceive them. They have standards far dif-ferent from those of people around them and are oblivious to how others respond to them. Whether the piggishness is chronic or occasional, it can be very dis-concerting when you are trying to focus on your work. It's also hard to treat your boss with the kind of respect you'd normally give someone in his position when his hair is greasy, his shirt is wrinkled, his office is filthy, and his shoes stink.

The most common strategy for dealing with Pigs is to try to ignore them. But, unfortunately, because every-one does just that, they never get the message about how bad they really are.

There are two ways to deal with a Pig Boss from Hell. Your approach should depend on what you think his level of awareness is. Is he oblivious to the problem, or is he aware of it but just doesn't think it's important?

Bosses can be unaware of bad breath, body odor, smelly shoes, or stale cigarette smoke. The problem could be dandruff, a crooked toupée, or bugs in his office.

The best way to deal with a boss unaware of a problem is to be direct but gentle. You want to correct the problem but keep the embarrassment factor to a minimum. You don't want him to become defensive, and you don't want to turn it into a big issue. Begin by acknowledging that it is an embarrassing subject. Let him know you are telling him because you respect him. Be plain and brief. Don't stay around too long after you break the news to him — it will just increase his embarrassment. Here's an example of how you might approach it:

> Boss, there's something I want to talk to you about. It's kind of embarrassing, and I don't really know how to bring it up, but . . . well . . . I don't think you notice it, but you have a bit of a body odor problem. It's not really horrible, but it is noticeable. I'm really sorry to bring it up like this, but, well, I have a lot of respect for you, and I thought I should tell you before it became a problem for you.

The manner in which you phrase the problem is paramount. On the one hand, you don't want to play it down so much that he does nothing about it; on the other hand, you don't want to come right out and say something that may come across as a personal insult.

Sometimes your boss is aware of his condition but

doesn't consider it important enough to deal with. It could be unwashed clothes, not bathing, or a filthy workplace, etc. In these cases, your strategy is to bring to his attention how sensitive other people are to what he is doing without leaving him feeling judged or condemned. The best way to do this is with a quick, offhand comment or observation.

- Hey, boss, is that the same shirt you wore yesterday?
- Is that last week's lunch on your desk?
- Didn't have time to iron this morning?

By making a simple comment, you are pointing out something to your boss that he didn't think other people paid attention to. Now that he knows other people have noticed, he'll likely make a change — quickly.

5. Pet Peeves

It doesn't seem to matter how hard everyone on her team works, this boss always has her "pet" employees. There are pets that she nurtures and others that she kicks. People who get all the breaks and special assignments and people who always seem to be scapegoats when things go wrong.

This Boss from Hell believes that, to enhance productivity, the best strategy is to play one employee against another. She makes sure that at any given time there is one employee in her good graces and another in the doghouse. It wouldn't be so bad if the message she was trying to send was a productive one — that if you work hard you will be rewarded and that if you don't work hard there will be consequences. But Pet Peeves seems to make her choices completely at random. One day you're the dog, the next you're the hydrant.

What makes her so frustrating is that she creates a pervasive sense of unfairness in the workplace. "What's the point of even trying?" you think to yourself. "Charlie's the one who's going to get the credit anyway." Even Charlie is uncomfortable with the situation.

When I was 19, I spent a summer working with a company that installed swimming pools. It was tough, manual labor and required a lot of teamwork to get the jobs done. Richard, the owner of the company, spent most of his time in his truck driving between work sites, checking up on his crews. In my third week, Richard pointed at me and said "You're with me." And, for the next two weeks, I rode with him in his truck to keep him company and did very little discernible work. While the easy job was certainly appealing, the discomfort it created between me and my coworkers was not. Even though they knew I hadn't asked for the cushy job, they couldn't help but feel slightly resentful about my special treatment.

It wasn't long before I asked Richard if it would be all right to get back to doing on-site work. At the end of his first day with Richard, the crew worker he'd replaced me with asked me what had possessed me to give up such an easy job. But two weeks later he, too, asked to resume his on-site work. It became a standing joke, and almost a badge of dishonor, to become what we began to refer to as "Richard's Pet."

A boss who has obvious pet employees rarely has any idea that her favoritism is having a negative impact on the workplace. And when she does perceive discomfort among other members of the team, instead of recognizing her role in creating the situation, she perceives it simply as her employees being petty. Perhaps the most important thing to remember is that, if the boss has a favorite, it's not necessarily the fault of the employee. Don't condemn him for your boss' actions.

It's unlikely that anything you do will prevent your boss from playing the favorites game. But it's important that she not begin to perceive you as petty or jealous. If she does, you may quickly find yourself at the top of her other list. Your best strategy is to stay quiet.

6. Kings and Queens

Some bosses we encounter consider themselves simply above it all. They are the rulers of their domains, and they go to tremendous lengths to ensure that everyone is aware that they are clearly not at the same level as you or I. They don't eat with the little people, they don't socialize with the little people, and they don't place a lot of weight in the things the little people say. They expect their employees to recognize how Very Important they really are and treat them accordingly. Those who have the audacity to do things suggesting an equal relationship are quickly corrected.

Sonya Plowman, now an editor of Caribbean travel magazines (tough job!), once shared this story with me:

I hadn't been at the job long – I'd landed the writer/researcher position maybe a month earlier. One day I went to work with a bad cold. I would have taken the day off, but we were close to deadline, and I knew my boss needed me there. So I went in, and sniffled away, until I spied a box of tissues on his desk, which I helped myself to. Sniff after sniff, sneeze after sneeze, I plucked at that tissue box. "Ahem," said my boss after a short time. "Those tissues are actually mine, not the company's – we don't provide tissues to our employees here."

One of my clients, in the fashion business, tells of her first fashion job and the time she had the opportunity to meet the Big Boss — a fashion guru from New York:

I was just an eager kid, excited to meet him. I put on my biggest smile, walked up to him, and introduced myself. "Hi, I'm Janet. I work for you here in the L.A. office."

"How very nice for you," he responded coolly, then turned his back on me to talk with someone else. I felt like a squashed bug. Clearly, I wasn't qualified to talk to him.

That common, and I believe misguided, theory that bosses should not get too close to their employees is taken to new heights by Kings and Queens. Not only do they believe that familiarity breeds contempt, but they also believe that any kind of interaction beyond giving orders is a sign of weakness. They are into status and very aware of the relative status of those around them. They aren't typically abusive or unreasonable — they're just an annoying blend of arrogance and condescension.

The best way to survive a King or Queen Boss from Hell is through elements of the FIRST approach outlined earlier in this book. Because of their self-proclaimed lofty position, it becomes easy to fly below their radar, and with the proper reframing they can become fairly easy to ignore. Both become much harder to do, however, if "arrogance" happens to be one of your hot buttons. You may find that your only other option is to look elsewhere for employment.

Whatever you do, resist the sometimes overwhelming temptation to try to "put them in their place" or knock them down a peg or two. This approach will have no effect and can often backfire. That devastating verbal barb you want to throw their way will never be felt because they give no credibility to the source. Any action you take will be perceived as trivial. If there is any consolation to working with Kings or Queens, it's that they usually end up being their own worst enemies. They have a tendency to self-destruct as their bosses and peers also become annoyed with their behavior.

7. The Boor

He is the poster boy for sensitivity training. He is the reason the increasingly annoying political correctness movement hasn't died long ago. He says grossly inappropriate things at inappropriate times. You can't help but believe that he's going out of his way — like Simon on *American Idol* — to hurt people's feelings. He is insensitive, tactless, rude, and uncaring.

I have a cousin who related this gem to me about a former boss: "He drinks too much at social events and embarrasses everyone by pointing out their personal weaknesses. He once asked a pregnant employee 'So when are you calving?'"

I had a boss many years ago who would comment constantly on people's weight. He once told an account executive that he didn't want him as a passenger in his car because he didn't have heavy-duty springs.

For people who have high self-esteem and a thicker skin, the Boor is typically no more than an unpleasant, annoying, but generally harmless intrusion into their lives. But for those who are very sensitive, or in the least bit insecure, the Boor can really begin to push buttons in a big way. His continual displays of disrespect wear quickly and can distract us from getting our work done.

The Boor is entirely self-focused. In some cases, his behavior is his way of communicating the power he holds. He's doing things against the social rules to send the message that he does, in fact, have the power to do them. When no one speaks out against him, he wins. When someone does take him to task, he also wins, since he quickly labels his attacker as being "hypersensitive."

Whatever the Boor does, the first rule is *don't react to it.* If you do or say something that he perceives as supporting his behavior, he will see you as a compatriot, and you'll be painted with the same brush as he is. If you react badly to his behavior, you become a target. The best strategy with the Boor is to use a little lighthearted sarcasm — not quite cutting enough to make him defensive, but strong enough to send a message. Whenever you hear him make a boorish comment, respond with a smile and a quick little comeback. Here are a few examples.

- Slow day in the niceness department today, boss?
- If only you could use that biting wit for goodness and niceness instead of evil.
- You should go on TV with that routine, boss – at least that way I could turn you off.

- Nothing like a little sexism in the morning to motivate the team, right, boss?
- Don't be yourself, boss, be nice.

Remember that his boorishness is a type of bullying. By responding with sarcasm, you send the message that you don't take either him or what he says seriously. That is not the response he is looking for.

8. Grumpy

Several years ago I met the owner of a number of automotive dealerships. He was tremendously successful on a financial level, but he was also one of the unhappiest individuals I have ever met. It's not that he was mean to his staff or rude to his customers. He wasn't particularly nasty. He was just in a continuous state of grumpiness.

When we told him the exciting news that the training program our company had conducted had increased his sales for the past two weeks by over 20%, he just looked over the top of his glasses at us, grunted, nodded his head, and went back to work. When I mentioned to the general manager of one of the dealerships that the owner didn't seem to be too happy about what we'd done, the general manager just laughed. "Oh, he was happy, all right — at least he was as happy as he ever gets. Heck, for him, that was a ringing endorsement! When he is unhappy, you'll be the first to know!"

It's easy to tell an environment managed by a grumpy boss. People are quiet and subdued. Furniture is old and worn. Equipment is as low-tech as possible. Grumpy rarely discusses anything but business, and even then he uses few words. Nobody has ever seen him smile, much less get excited over something.

The Grumpy boss, despite outward appearances, is usually a very decent person. He's kind of like a chocolate truffle — hard and crusty on the outside, soft and mushy on the inside. He is very sensitive but has spent a lifetime controlling his emotions. Although he will never admit it, he has a well-developed sense of humor, and he enjoys being around people who are enthusiastic. He hates to be around people who are as grumpy as he is.

The best way to work with a Grumpy boss is to challenge him. Have fun with him. Tease him. And when you do it, watch his eyes. You'll see the smile deep within them. One of my first bosses fell into the category of Grumpy, and everyone was intimidated by him. There was a sparkle in his eye, however, and I learned to have a lot of fun with him. I'll never forget sitting in a meeting with him (the president) and a gaggle of vice-presidents and directors. I was giving a report on one of our client's activities when he interrupted me with a growl.

"Surely they aren't expecting us to have this finished within a week!"

Looking right at him, with as straight a face as I

could muster, I fired back, "Oh, we'll have it done. . . . And don't call me Shirley."

No one quite knew what to say. But through the moment of silence, I could see my boss's face mildly contorting as he tried to hold back a smile. Apparently, after I left, one of the vps began to bluster about my "blatant disrespect," to which my boss grumbled "Am I the only one with a sense of humor around here?"

No one, not even Grumpy bosses, has ever fired someone for being too happy, too enthusiastic, or too motivated. Remember that. If he gets on your nerves, kill him with kindness.

There are many other kinds of Bosses from Hell, of course. I'm not sure it would be possible to catalog all of the types. But these are the ones we see most often. Some of the more severe types, such as Sexual Harassers, Physical Abusers, Bigots, and Racists, I chose not to include. These are extremely serious issues that require very serious action, and if you encounter them you shouldn't hesitate to bring in other people — lawyers, the police, etc. I think you'll find, though, that the strategies I've presented will help you to deal with most of the other Boss from Hell types you are likely to encounter.

GIVE 'EM HELL

Don't permit yourself a victim mentality. Don't give up your power. Don't let anything or anyone stand in the way of your destiny.

How many Bosses from Hell does it take to screw in a lightbulb? Two. One to hold the whip while he makes you screw it in, and the other to rant that you're not doing a good enough job. There are days, when you're dragging your butt out of bed, wondering if you should even bother going into work at all, when that's exactly the way work seems to be.

You might think, from reading this book, that Bosses from Hell are rampant, raging lunatics who are an unavoidable part of life. That's not really the case. One important thing to remember is that not all bosses are like the ones discussed here. In fact, the Boss from Hell, while maybe very real to you at the moment, truly represents only a small fraction of the bosses out there. The vast majority of bosses are decent people, fair and kind to their employees. They care about doing a good, honest job, and they care about the people who work for them. What we've covered in this book are the exceptions.

If nothing else, I hope I've been able to communicate that most of the Bosses from Hell you'll encounter are just ordinary people like you and me. They simply don't manage very well, that's all. They are underskilled and undermotivated people with hopes, dreams, fears, and frailties. They aren't born with some evil boss gene. They, like us, want to be successful. The encouraging part is that most of them, with the proper handling, can be made at least tolerable.

Having said this, never forget that, like most people, you'll probably spend over half of your adult life at work. The question you have to keep asking yourself is "For such a large chunk of my life, is 'tolerable' good enough?" If your answer is "No," then you have to take a close look at what you're doing, and at whom you're doing it with, and start building yourself a better life.

But before you run off in search of that perfect boss and that perfect job, make sure that you first take a good look at yourself. Try to identify what you can do to make your current situation better. Try to identify how much of the grief is actually being created, or made worse, by your own actions. I'll never forget one seminar participant who came up to me during a break in a team-building exercise. He told me that this was his sixth job in the past 10 years and that in every job he'd worked for a Boss from Hell. Maybe I was being cynical, but it seemed to me that the problem might not have been with his bosses. If you find yourself in a similar situation, a little introspection may help you to point your finger in the right direction.

Finally, and most importantly, don't ever lose sight of how much real control you have over your own destiny and how much more you might be able to get out of your workplace by taking positive, proactive steps. Don't permit yourself a victim mentality. Don't give up your power. Don't let anything or anyone stand in the way of your destiny.

Someone once said "Life is not a dress rehearsal." I can't think of a better mantra for living your life. Every moment of every hellish workday that passes is lost to you forever when you don't take steps to make things better. And if there is one thing that you don't want your Boss from Hell to take from you, it's your future.